ONE FOOT IN HEAVEN

One Foot in
Heaven

The Life of a Practical Parson

BY

HARTZELL SPENCE

Illustrated by Donald McKay

GROSSET & DUNLAP

<small>PUBLISHERS</small>   NEW YORK

By arrangement with McGraw-Hill Book Company, Inc.

PUBLISHED BY WHITTLESEY HOUSE

A division of the McGraw-Hill Book Company, Inc.

Printed in the United States of America

To Mother

ONE FOOT IN HEAVEN

I

❧ ◊ ❧

ON PALM SUNDAY, my father was preaching a particularly resounding sermon. The church was packed, and father warmed to a responsive house like an old trouper playing Hamlet's gravedigger.

His text was the third chapter of John 7–10, which he had read out in the simplified Weymouth translation: "Do not be astonished at my telling you, 'You must all be born anew.' The wind blows where it chooses, and you hear its sound, but you do not know where it comes from or where it is going. So is it with everyone who has been born of the spirit."

Palm Sunday was the climax of my father's pastoral year, leading as it did into Holy Week. Father put all his might into the Palm Sunday sermon—the sermon he had pointed toward all during Lent—and followed it up on Good Friday with Holy Communion. This was *his* day. On Easter, he did not try to compete against the choir and the new hats. So he was dusting off his doctrine of rebirth with all the forthrightness in him, which was considerable, and was just stretching up toward the magnificent climax of an altar call when an usher tiptoed

[3]

to the pulpit and whispered in his ear. Father finished his sentence, closed his Psalter with a slap, and broke at once into his benediction. Even this he shortened.

"The Lord bless thee and keep thee, Amen," he said and ducked out the side door. But ritual, even in a crisis, was strongly upon him, and he called back over his shoulder: "We will dispense with the closing hymn."

By the time the stunned twelve hundred communicants had recovered their poise, father was rattling up the hill in his old Ford, with the motor wide open, his eyes fixed grimly on the hilltop where our house was burning as heartily as any sinner in Hell.

That was my father. He was practical.

Being a Methodist, father in principle was faithful to the rigid tenets of John Wesley and the Methodist Discipline. We lived by the Discipline. Sometimes we well-nigh ate it, too; for no one who ever lived on a Methodist minister's salary will doubt the miracle of manna from Heaven. It came from Heaven, or we starved. In rules of conduct, he was as stern as any circuit rider. We of his household balanced, precarious Christians, with one foot in Heaven and one on earth, not daring to plant both feet solidly either way. The happy heathen ranged the earth and foraged well; the good church deacons, secure in their salvation, had nothing to worry about except the spiritual shortcomings of others—mainly the preacher and his family. But we, examples of the Good Faith on this earth, righteously preparing for a land we weren't sure we'd like a bit, toed a narrow mark neither Heavenly nor earthly. I knew, but never said, where we were: it was Hell.

Father was as strict as anybody about card playing and dancing and low-necked dresses and short skirts and other works of the Devil. Now and again he would preach a sermon on the prophecies of Isaiah that would curl the hair on the heads of his parishioners.

But he knew that an austere text, even from the teachings of Jesus, should not be carried too far. He never took literally the admonition from the Sermon on the Mount: "If thy right arm cause thee to stumble, cut it off." Father had no desire for a church full of left-handed worshipers. Some of them looked bad enough from the pulpit as it was. And too narrow an interpretation of this particular doctrine would have ruined his appeal, on missionary Sundays, for the people to dig into their money pocket with *both* hands. He was practical, all right.

He had to be. For his church rarely attracted the wealthy of the Episcopalians and Congregationalists or the scrupulously tithing faithful of the Baptists or the consistently generous of the Roman Catholic faith. Father used to say he knew well what Benjamin Franklin meant when he called people "as poor as church mice." Poor Richard was letting the Methodist Society have it between the eyes.

Father carried over his personal beliefs into the recreation of his children. When other youngsters were out on Sunday afternoon playing run sheep run, my sister Eileen and I were indoors under father's watchful eye, idling over a game we had received at Christmas from the Methodist Book Concern. It consisted of matching verses in the Bible with their authors.

My sister would read from a card: "For God so loved the world . . . " and I would reply smartly, "John 3:

16." When we wearied of this game, father would set us to memory work from the Bible: the Temptations, the Sermon on the Mount, the Psalms of David, and such isolated inspirational guidance as II Timothy 2:15 and I Thessalonians 5:11–22.

I could never understand why this mental and spiritual exercise was better than playing marbles on the school grounds across the street, providing I didn't play for "keeps." But father always had an answer to that.

"Go and learn the 119th Psalm," he would say, "from the 105th to the 112th lines, inclusive." To this day I can recite it, recalling at the same time the tempting shouts of neighbor children through the open window. "Thy word is a lamp unto my feet, and light unto my path. I have sworn and have confirmed it, that I will observe Thy righteous ordinances. . . . The wicked have laid a snare for me; yet have I not gone astray from Thy precepts."

All else failing and the weather being particularly sinful with the temptations of early spring, father would gather us around the piano.

"Remember the Nineteenth Psalm?" he would ask hopefully.

Usually my sister did, if I didn't, and she would respond dutifully: "The Heavens declare the glory of God, and the firmament showeth His handiwork."

"Good," father would say and strike a heavy chord. "This hymn is by Isaac Watts. I told you about his life long ago. Let us sing."

And sing we did, until we had committed to memory all six verses, father joining in a magnificent voice that was neither baritone nor tenor, but with the range of both and a tonal quality that made up in faith what it lacked in timbre.

> The Heavens declare Thy glory, Lord;
> In every star Thy wisdom shines;
> But when our eyes behold Thy word
> We read Thy name in fairer lines.

There was a fierce serenity about father's whole figure as he sang, the triumph of Heaven in his chords and a defiance in his eyes that said: "You'll learn this hymn, or I'll tan the living daylight out of you." He would have, too.

Yet father accepted humorously the shortcomings of his parish.

One day on his parochial rounds he called on a maiden lady of forty-six who for years had dominated the women's societies. A true daughter of Dorcas, her hand was in every missionary barrel, every poor box, every gossip pot. Her name went up to Conference every year as the president of something—sometimes of the Ladies' Aid, often of the Home Missionary society, and occasionally of the Sew and So club.

This year Miss Martha was president of the Woman's Foreign Missionary society, and she had been ill for a week. The two circumstances were related, as father learned when he stopped by, ready as usual to pray at her bedside if that was necessary or to jolly her along if need be. He found Miss Martha well blanketed in bed.

"I'm low, Brother Spence," she responded to his greeting.

Miss Martha was a true sister of Methodism, and she

insisted on using the church's familiar form of salutation. But father used it only when first so addressed.

"And why should you be low, sister?"

"It's—it's—" She turned away her head.

Father, who had studied medicine in college and knew when one of his flock was merely enjoying an illness, looked down at her kindly.

"Your trouble is of the spirit, then, not of the body?"

Miss Martha nodded.

"Perhaps if you were to be fortified by prayer—" father began. He knew the real nature of the complaint of many neurotic maiden ladies. Often I heard him tell mother, after visiting sisters like Miss Martha, "What she needs is a husband—'most any man would do."

But this day Miss Martha was not suffering from her usual affliction.

"Don't pray for me," she interrupted, "pray for Sister Hastings. She *needs* it."

Father nodded gravely. He had encountered the rivalry of Miss Martha and Mrs. Hastings the day we arrived in town, when Mrs. Hastings' chocolate cake reached the parsonage ahead of Miss Martha's pumpkin pie.

"She's a sinful woman," Miss Martha went on bitterly. "She says things no Christian woman would even think. Why, do you know—"

"Ah," father interrupted, "yes, indeed. Isn't Sister Hastings treasurer of the Foreign Missionary society?"

"Why, yes."

"Then she's got a right to do a little sinning," said father. "I doubt even the Lord would ask a woman to be a Christian and a missionary treasurer at the same time."

[8]

That was father. His remark was not meant to be blasphemous or facetious. It was practical Christianity: to nip with humorous shock a feminine quarrel that might otherwise cause trouble. Many stories of father's ministry remained behind in each town he served, and all were lovingly told. To keep Protestants in church at all requires far more than an earnest preaching of the will of God.

To be worth his salt, a preacher must be sincerely pious, narrow to the point of bigotry in his private life, a master politician with both his parish and the higher church organization, and a financial juggler just one step up the Heavenly ladder from Wall Street. Above all, he must have a quick wit, the courage of a first-century martyr, and a stomach that will not complain of meager rations. If he possesses these qualities and a wife who will neither offend anyone nor outshine her husband, he is eligible for a country parish.

To climb to a city pulpit, he must have still other qualifications: an unimpeachable respect for his own ability, the oratorical fire of Savonarola, the organizational genius of a minority politician, a society doctor's bedside manner, and, if possible, a couple of sons studying for the ministry. If, in addition, he is adept at flattery, he may eventually become a bishop.

But my father had no desire to be a bishop. He went to the church's General Conferences and, when necessary, pulled strings to bring about the election of bishops who would give him what he wanted. He preferred even a small salary from a single church to the uncertain stipend of the bishop, eked from the lean tills of all the charges in the bishop's area. But more than that, he considered stardom a personal tragedy.

"Many a man," he would say, "has been so dazzled by his own light that he could not find his way."

Never could he be enticed away from a parsonage even to be a district superintendent or president of a Methodist college, although these posts were offered to him. He had undertaken the Lord's work, and work at it he would in the vineyard that needed the heartiest labor: the town parish.

Even when he had the opportunity to become a bishop in northern India, he declined, saying, "The real heathen are not outside the church but in it, and to them will I be missionary."

In only one particular did father sidestep the rigid Discipline of his church. The printed Methodist rules strictly forbade sartorial elegance, and father was vain about his clothes.

And well he might be, for he had a figure to hang them on: six feet one inch of military erectness, magnificent shoulders, his whole body vibrantly proud to be in the army of the Lord. The words of "Onward Christian Soldiers" leaped at you when father entered a room. The first impression you received was of proud physical strength. But this vanished when you looked into father's eyes—the eyes of one who, from the beginning, has envisioned a purpose and still visions it, though the purpose has been achieved. They were the eyes of a believer, firmly planted in the rock. Yet in their hazel gray were kindliness and compassion, and a twinkle that caused him difficulty with certain maiden ladies.

He was to the women in his churches what a matinee

Idol is to movie-goers. Constantly he had to be on guard. In every parish there were homes into which he dared not go alone. Now and then a feminine church member became so enamored of him that he was embarrassed. In such cases he appealed to mother. Sometimes she helped to extricate him, but there were occasions when she let him squirm out of his predicament by himself.

Despite his elegance, however, father carried himself with such dignity that no one ever accused him of being a dandy. He never showed off his clothes; he just wore them. And his appearance was a definite asset in the midst of Methodist austerity. One churchgoer at Fort Dodge, Iowa, wrote her husband:

"Our new pastor is a Man of God who can walk the earth and yield not an inch to any man. He is a parson with pride enough in his God to dress up for Him, which he most certainly does. At the reception we went to gape at his clothes, and remained to fall under the spell of his word. Everyone is very much pleased, for he looks like a lot more salary than he is getting. Half the girls are already planning church weddings, Mr. Spence in his cutaway coat would fit in so perfectly. They'd better be careful, though, because I'm afraid Mr. Spence would outshine the groom." She was right, too. Father often outshone the bride herself.

Children were particularly attracted to him, and he was most magnetic when, in his quiet study, the probationers gathered about him to hear his explanations of church dogma and Biblical admonition. Then he could make Christianity what for him it was: the end and all of living, now and forever, Amen. Those who became infected never lost the virus. Twenty years after her

[11]

confirmation as a girl of twelve, a woman told me: "It is blasphemous to say it, but since your father put me through my catechism, my religion has been the memory of your father. To this day I can't say where God begins and your father leaves off."

In voice father was powerful and persuasive. Although ordinarily he preached conversationally, without ranting or shouting, he could tremble the rafters of the biggest auditorium when necessary.

He was a salesman of God's word, and he sold it with all his might: by word and deed, by voice and appearance, by threats and cajolery, by fire and compassion. But he got it sold. And his converts stayed sold. During the entire course of his ministry, he never left a parish with less than a twenty-five per cent net increase in membership, nor after the first few weeks did he preach to less than a comfortably full house.

He was one clergyman of whom it was never said: "In the morning the church was not quite full, and in the evening it was not quite empty."

2

‏❧

FATHER was pulled into the ministry.

He had planned to be a physician in his native Canada and studied with that idea in view. But during his senior year in the University of Toronto he went one night to a Methodist revival to hear spellbinding old Bishop Hartzell, for whom I am named.

The spell was working that night. It caught father and held him. Impressionable, burning with zeal to help his fellow man as he thought only a doctor could, his fire stoked by a Celtic imagination and a Scottish nobility of purpose, he listened to the bishop's confidence in the compassion of God and leaped to his feet at the first invitation. He was converted: as the Methodists understand conversion. The Lord personally placed a hand on his shoulder, and father accepted the Call. Never once thereafter was he in doubt. He always knew that in the ministry he had found everything he would have experienced in medicine, and much, much more.

Having decided to become a preacher, he yearned to begin his lifework quickly. He needed no further education, for he had majored in philosophy and had then spent four years at medical school. His scholastic equipment far outstripped the requirements.

"You can catch up on your homiletics as you go along," the bishop said when, two weeks after his conversion, father announced his intention.

"All right," father replied. "Where do I start?"

The population of Canada was static at that time. No new churches were being built, and all the available pastorates were filled. This Bishop Hartzell explained.

"But I can't wait for dead men's shoes," father protested. "I taught school six years before I went to college. Now I'm twenty-nine years old. I have to get started."

The bishop suggested Iowa, a growing country where a career awaited young men. But in Canadian thinking the United States was a "jumping-off place," inhabited only by rascals and cattle thieves. A migration from Ontario to Iowa was almost unthinkable. Still, the jump was no greater than from the operating room to the pulpit. So father decided to jump.

"All right," Bishop Hartzell said, "I'll arrange with the Iowa bishop to place you in September. What's your full name?"

As Bishop Hartzell sat down to fill out the usual records, father thought fast. Christened William Spence, he had been sensitive for years because he had no middle name. Now the dignity of a religious career seemed to require a stabilizing second initial. He appropriated one.

"William H Spence," he said. But when he signed the application, he was careful not to put a dot after the "H."

Father lingered in Toronto only long enough to get a diploma. Then he hurried to see his fiancée in Stratford, Ontario. When he told her that he had reorganized his life and was going to Iowa as a preacher instead of settling in Canada as a doctor, the words of Ruth, "Your people shall be my people, and your God, my God," came home to her with a very personal impact. But his life was her life, and her only concern was for his family.

"What," she asked gently, "will your father say to your becoming a Yankee?"

Thoughtfully father went home to the farm near New-bridge, Ontario, and put his decision to his parents. They were surprised, not so much by his shift in career as by his plan to go far away. This son had been ordering his own life since, at the age of sixteen, he had turned his back on the soil and had set out for Stratford to educate himself for a professional career.

"All right," my grandfather said, "you certainly are old enough to know what you are doing. My father was just your age when he left Scotland for the new world. His decision was for the best. Perhaps yours is, too."

That was June 1, 1904.

Three months later, when North Iowa's rolling prairies were heavy with harvest, father stepped alone from a train at Laketon, wondering what he was in for and where to begin. He saw at a glance that the town was small, with a muddy main street, three churches, and the homes of a few merchants and retired farmers.

A fat man who had been looking out the meat-market window scraped suet from his hands and rushed across the street.

"You the new preacher?" he asked.

"Yes," answered father, setting down a shining new Gladstone bag.

"I'm George Reynolds, and ma says to bring you up

to the house to take the weight off your feet. From the looks of you, I'd say it was considerable weight."

"One eighty-five," said father, "and every pound of it happy to meet you, Brother Reynolds. I didn't expect a welcome."

"That torture comes later," Reynolds remarked, a gleam in his eye. "Come along." Without bothering to lock his shop, he started up the street with the new minister in tow. "This here," he explained, pointing into the hardware store, "belongs to Brother Sylvester. A cantankerous old critter and a devil. He runs the church, but don't you cross him. He pays most of your salary."

Father nodded thoughtfully.

"And this," Reynolds went on, "is Sister McClintock's bakery. She's head of the Ladies' Aid. Don't go in now, or we'll be there all day. Up this way . . . "

They turned into a street lined with hard maple trees.

"Over there's the blacksmith shop. That's Brother Turnipseed's."

"Brother who?"

"Turnipseed," Reynolds repeated, as matter-of-factly as he would have cut a pork chop from a lean loin. "Odd name, all right. There's lots of turnips been sown in these parts, and good seed, too. Best workers in the church. You'll get more of 'em, out and around."

And father did. In two years he learned to respect a clan generous and loyal, and better singers than most of the choir.

He was still thinking about this strange name when Reynolds pushed him unceremoniously into an alley.

"Sorry, brother," he apologized, "but I got orders to bring the new parson home, and I can't risk losing you to

Sister Watkins. She was a comin' at us with a full-head of steam, and if she'd ever got here we'd never get home to dinner."

He ducked in a gate and called back a warning.

"Mind your head. That trumpet vine wasn't built for no six-footer."

They went in through the kitchen.

"Meet ma," the butcher said, and pointed.

Ma was taking an apple pie from the oven. Her hair was down over her eyes, her face burned red from the heat of the coal range, and her apron was a copious suggestion of everything she had been cooking.

Without even looking up, she scolded, "George, the very idea, bringing anybody in through the back—"

Then she saw the elegance of father and stopped.

"Oh my law," she gasped and stood spellbound, the hot pie still in her hands.

She looked him up and down, and her eyes sparkled at the tailored coat of fine black broadcloth and the wing collar that sat so proudly upon father, as though knowingly showing off something handsome. She darted a quick, embarrassed look at her husband's open throat and compared it with the newcomer's polka-dotted tie and star-sapphire stickpin. Then she recalled, in confusion, her own appearance.

"Goodness," she stammered, a blush almost purpling her fiery complexion. Then she rallied long enough to put the pie on the table.

Father tried to reassure her with eyes that saw only the woman's inner geniality, but it was an experience he never forgot. At that moment he learned his first ministerial lesson: a sister of the parish hates to be caught

[17]

unprepared by her preacher. Ever after, on pastoral rounds, he lingered out front tying his horse (or, in later years, testing the soundness of his automobile tires) until a flick of the window curtain told him he had been seen. Then he would saunter to the door, admiring the hawthorn or the apple tree until ample time had elapsed for his hostess to whisk off her apron and shove the baby's toys out of sight down the basement stairs.

Mrs. Reynolds now glanced gratefully at her guest for pretending not to notice her discomfiture and shrugged her broad shoulders.

"Well," she said, "you might as well see me at my worst, I do declare."

Father followed up his advantage.

"A woman cooking up such heavenly aromas as I smell is the best sight you could show me. Brother Reynolds praised your cooking all the way down the street, and he was so anxious for me to see it with my own eyes that we took a short cut in the back way."

That remark was worth many a free chunk of calves' liver in later days. George brightened, and ma beamed.

"Well," she laughed, "there are those who say I'm a good cook, if you'll forgive me for forgetting my humility. At least, I notice the preacher comes oftener to dinner at my house than to most."

Father, delighted at what appeared to be spontaneous hospitality on the part of the Reynoldses, now discovered it had an ulterior motive. They were not just being nice to him; they good-naturedly wanted him to accept their ideas of how the church should be run before anyone else in town could influence him. He learned the shortcomings of the parish, whom the Reynoldses thought he should be on guard against, and their attitude on every church dispute. Had he been a man of prejudices, he would have left the Reynolds house suspicious of everyone in town except his host and hostess.

"It seems," he wrote his prospective bride that night, "that they who labor in the vineyard of the Lord have conflicting views on the best method of harvest. Today I have learned one side of many controversies; doubtless I'll discover a good many others." And he did.

The parish proved to be an active one, ideal for training a young man in his lifework. It was what is known as a circuit, a holdover from the previous half century, when the only Christian ministry available was provided by itinerant preachers who sometimes attended a dozen congregations. By 1904, when father arrived, the area had been condensed to the town of Laketon and two rural parishes. But the limitation in area had not decreased activity. The trend was toward more people in less space, and the minister had a fast-growing population to care for.

Father's headquarters were in town, and there he preached on Sunday morning. Then, after dinner with one of his members (he quickly learned which sisters were the best cooks), he would hitch up his horse and go to one of the country charges for an afternoon sermon, returning to town for an evening service. During the week he had sermons to write, babies to baptize, sickbeds to sit beside, midweek prayer meetings to lead, couples to marry, people to bury, studying to do, men's and women's organizations to direct, young people to guide, and a business to keep going in three churches. He was on call twenty-four hours a day.

For three months he worked alone, then confessed to

himself that he needed help. So he disappeared. That was on Monday. When he returned on Saturday, he brought a wife. He gave the Laketon congregation only a few hours' warning: a telegram from Chicago to Mr. McCreery, his only wealthy parishioner.

"Now, Hope," father boomed excitedly as the train stopped at Laketon's little red station, "I'll prove there's nobody out here to scalp you except the congregation."

He plunged toward the vestibule, his arms full of luggage. But mother detained him.

"You'd better be more discreet now, dear," she said. "You've been talking in a very loud voice the whole trip. In fact, you haven't stopped since we were married." Seeing his hurt look, she sought to give him an impression he would remember and profit by ever after. "I don't think you married me because you loved me at all," she went on serenely. "I think it was just to have someone to talk to."

But the remark made no impression on father. He was probably born talking. Rarely during his waking hours was his voice quiet. He talked to himself while shaving; he read aloud. For years he followed mother about her housework, narrating his difficulties, testing his sermons, or just talking.

He introduced mother to Mr. McCreery, who met the train with a rubber-tired carriage drawn by matched bays and proudly noted Mr. McCreery's admiration of his bride, who was very pretty in a brown tailor-made suit with a fur-lined coat. When they were invited to the McCreery home for breakfast, father knew just how deep an impression mother had made. He had been anxious that mother's introduction to Laketon should be in the finest house in the county. But the day was not to end as smoothly as it began.

Arrival of the preacher with a bride caused great excitement. Such an event, of course, called for a reception. It also called for opening of the parsonage. So, as a bridegroom, father learned the next two painful lessons of his ministry: that nothing can be as much torture as a church social event or anything quite so un-Christian as a church parsonage.

These crimes were perpetrated on father and mother simultaneously. Since he had given no advance warning, the Parsonage Aid society had no time to give the church manse an overhauling. So when Mr. McCreery, after breakfast, drove the pastor and his bride to their future home, the shock was devastating. Mother, freshly beautiful and straight from her own fine home and gracious living, paled as she entered. It was not only ugly but dirty. Usually parsonages are terribly shabby and miserably located. But, as a rule, they are clean when a new minister moves in. The Laketon house would have been immaculate, too, if the church had had any intimation that its bachelor pastor had gone away for a bride. Mother wandered from room to room, speechlessly, swallowing hard to fight back the tears.

"I was sick to my stomach," she said many years later.

Father's stomach was in better shape, fortified by three months of boardinghouse food and the new responsibilities of a bridegroom.

How bad the place really was I don't know. The memory of it softened through the years—and after life in other parsonages. But, to quote father: "It looked like a place the county poor farm had abandoned. A yellow dog wouldn't have lived in it. A cat wouldn't have been caught dead under the front porch. The moths starved to death there, and the mice smothered in its dust. The wallpaper in the front room looked like cuttings from a geranium bed. The rest of the house had no paper at all. The bedroom was too small to snore in comfortably, and the stairs were so narrow we wouldn't have been able to get up or down except that we were half starved. The kitchen, however, was big enough for a rich man's funeral."

The furniture was equally sorry. It consisted mainly of castoffs from the parlors, bedrooms, and woodsheds of a humble parish. The living room was dominated by an ominously big bookcase that was to loom even larger when father's few books were deposited in it. On the floor was a rag rug, presumably the handiwork of the Ladies' Aid. Father looked at its grime and exclaimed with a grin, "Well, at least we have a sample of all the germs in town."

The attic was full of old hats, shoes without laces, boxes of mementoes of previous pastoral penury, and some old love letters that father wouldn't let mother read. The basement was even worse. All the litter of a basement A.D. 1904 was in it, and more.

"Gaze in wonder," father said, more for something to say than for any other reason. "Look at this junk."

Mother looked.

"Now, here's something," he went on, "that you can profit by. Notice that a minister never throws anything away."

He kicked aside a ratty old coat and held up a battered shoe.

"You never know when these things will come in handy. That coat doesn't look like much now, but you may see it with different eyes another year, and by the end of the winter this shoe may look better than the ones I have on. Here's some more," he began rummaging gleefully in an old barrel. "You know, dear, I think the previous pastor, God bless him, left this stuff here on purpose. He knew this was my first charge, and I'll bet a hat he left these old relics for us to *use!*"

The Laketon circuit paid its pastor $385 a year—if he could collect it. And from the look of that attic, he rarely succeeded.

There was no bathroom, of course. When father wanted a bath, mother heated a teakettle on the big kitchen range and retired discreetly to her sewing. Father came in, set a washtub on the floor, poured in hot and cold water, and sponged. For ablutions of the inner man, there was an annex out by the alley.

Had mother been able to roll up her sleeves and go to work on that house, she might soon have made it livable —with her dowry silver, china, linen, and many other personal possessions. But the good women of the parish were in and out all day long. First they descended on the house and cleaned it with whirlwind energy and amazing skill. Then, one by one, they slipped away to return, an hour or two later, still embarrassed by the dirt mother had seen, with offerings of cookies and jam to make amends.

But each time they came, they made sure mother had not removed a favorite picture from its favorite spot on a wall or rolled that hideous rag rug into a bundle and hauled it to the attic. Thus mother realized that the parsonage belongs to the church women, who have definite ideas about its maintenance. They will battle to prevent removal of an ugly picture and resist equally strenuously the expenditure of two dollars to fix a hole in the roof that allows rain to drip on their pastor's bed.

Tired, dejected, and confused, mother was about to go to bed without bothering with dinner, when Mrs. McClintock rushed into the house with two loaves of bread.

"I'm awfully sorry I couldn't come sooner," she said, "but there was no one to mind the bakery. I'll make amends, though, by having a good talk with you at the reception tonight."

She looked at the clock, which had been given to the parsonage by her late husband and which no one since had found courage to remove from the mantel.

"Goodness," she exclaimed, "it's past six, and I must rush along, but I'll see you over at the church in an hour."

Mother sank with a sigh into the nearest chair.

"Oh, Will," she asked, "do we have to go out *tonight?*"

"I'm afraid, dear," father answered, weary, too, "that we must. I should have forewarned you, but the truth is, I forgot. Perhaps, though," he smiled, hopefully, "it will not last very long." He was disappointed; it continued for three agonizing hours.

The church reception is an inquisition that introduces a preacher and his family to a new parish. The women attend to discover whether the preacher's wife is strong-willed enough to override the clique that runs the Ladies' Aid. The men come to needle the new cleric into giving them places on the board of stewards or to protect the positions they already hold. The children, however, come only to eat the ice cream and cake that are as inevitable as the pastor's words of grace that precede their consumption.

The preacher, his wife and children, if any, line up before the door in the path of the strongest draught and are introduced to each member of the congregation by the church "boss." This dignitary is the self-appointed custodian of church affairs, and, to maintain his position, he pays more to church support than any other member. You can spot this individual the moment you walk into church on Sunday. He is the head usher. If there are folding doors between the Sunday-school room and the church auditorium, he rolls them back and forth. When the organ prelude starts, he steps to the altar to rearrange the flowers. During the service he gets up to open and shut windows. At the offertory he deals out the collection plates to the ushers, like a poker sharper with a cold deck. After church he stands at the side door and shakes hands with all who duck out that way rather than greet the pastor at the main portals.

On reception night, as chairman of the committee on pastoral relations, he introduces the new preacher. Father, having been in the parish for three months, knew everyone. But Brother Sylvester exercised his prerogative nonetheless.

For an hour and a half he kept father and mother standing by the door, vulnerable to every December blast, while he introduced the flock.

"Sister Reynolds, your preacher *and* his blushing bride."

Mother probably never blushed in her life. I never knew her to lose her self-control in public, not even at my father's funeral. Therefore, she resented being called a blushing bride, especially when Brother Sylvester used

[25]

the phrase for the hundred and fiftieth time without variation. The chill winter air beat her on one side, the Franklin stove baked her on the other, and her feet tortured her, but she managed to keep her smile genuine.

"My husband has told me so much of you," she would say, having been hurriedly coached by father beforehand, or "Yes, indeed. Will has written me of your good work with the children." One slip, one person slighted, one bit of praise misplaced, and her value in that parish was ended.

Then another hour of standing, backed now into cold corners by women with axes to grind or questions to ask. Would she teach a Bible class or help in the nursery? Could she sing? The choir badly needed an alto. Would she attend the next Woman's Home Missionary meeting if Mrs. Spicer dropped round in her new phaeton? Did she like the pickles Mrs. Ehrlich sent over by her hired girl? A score of dreamy-eyed maidens remarked, "You are so lucky, marrying Brother Spence. We have all learned to love him."

The minister's bride met them all, talked to all, and heard about their children, their aches and pains, and the price of a two-pound beef roast, "which you'd think Brother Reynolds, a member of our very own church, would give us a little cheaper than he gives it to the Lutherans!" Now and again she darted a feeble glance at father, begging for rescue. But he was having his own troubles, precariously balancing in one hand a dish of ice cream that melted before he could get a bite while he shook hands with the other. And he loved ice cream.

The reception broke up only when the fire died down and the children turned cranky. Then the parson bundled

up his bride and almost carried her across the street to the drab, cold parsonage.

She sank down on the shabby sofa, tears in her eyes.

"Another evening like this," she sobbed, "will kill me."

Father leaned down and kissed her.

"But this is just the beginning," he said huskily. "This is just the Laketon congregation. The two churches out on the circuit will have their receptions next week."

Remembering father's description of the six-mile ride home behind a pokey horse from the circuit churches, mother broke down completely and had to be carried to bed. There she stayed for five days. The circuit congregations were disappointed, of course, but not defeated. They sent sympathetic little notes and said they would be glad to postpone their receptions until mother felt better.

3

⤙♥⤚

By the time William Howard Taft was President, we were living in Fort Dodge, Iowa, and I was old enough to be patted on the head when he came to town to visit Senator Dolliver. My sister was old enough so that she wouldn't let Taft pat her head.

Five years had passed since father's arrival at Laketon, and he was able to write Bishop Hartzell, now retired:

"I have been moved this year to Fort Dodge. It is a great parish, with much to be done. It is the only Methodist church in a town of twelve thousand, and has nearly six hundred members, including Senator Dolliver. The church building is so old that it is infested with pigeons, but is excellently located two blocks from the main business street. The salary is magnificent: $2,400, but the parsonage is, as usual, a dingy place, right next door to the church, handy for borrowing. Sometimes I think that in building their churches, the Methodists are more careful to bring the parsonage kitchen within easy borrowing range, than they are to have the pulpit visible from the pews. But it is a large and important church, and I am looking forward eagerly to my pastorate here."

The bishop had been keeping an eye on his protégé from afar, but even he was surprised that a man so young should have reached the second-best church in the Conference. He wrote the district superintendent for particulars.

The following is part of the reply:

"Brother Spence is truly a remarkable young man, but is fomenting in the Conference the dangerous sin of jealousy. Half the brethren are on his side, the other half green with envy, so that Conference is no longer the spiritual reinforcement it should be. Brother Spence has learned how to get what he wants, a secret our other pastors would like much to learn. Last year he had his eyes on Fort Dodge, but was turned down at Conference on grounds of his youth. This was the only possible pretext the Bishop could find, for his competence both as preacher and pastor are becoming celebrated throughout the whole northwest, and he is much in demand as a Commencement orator in the high schools. During the summer a strange thing happened. Several members of the Fort Dodge congregation who had heard our good brother's Commencement address in their town, went up to Clarion to hear Brother Spence preach. A month before Conference, the Fort Dodge church asked Bishop S—— to appoint Brother Spence to their charge, in such a manner that he could not refuse. Everyone suspects the fine hand of Brother Spence in all this, but of course there is no proof."

The suspicion was correct. Father had learned to nail down his appointments ahead of time. This was possible because of the peculiar governing structure of the

Methodist church, which operates on a Conference system.

These Conferences start in the individual church. Four times a year the district superintendent, a sort of ecclesiastical top sergeant, comes to town and presides at a business meeting. The fourth of these Quarterly Conferences is the most important, since it falls in September, when all books must be balanced for the fiscal year. If the church does not like its preacher, the district superintendent is informed.

The reason all books are closed in September is that the Conference meets in the autumn. This is a general session of all the pastors over a wide area, in father's case, at that time, the Northwest Iowa Conference. Lay delegates also attend, elected by their own churches, their number depending on the size of the parish. Throughout the week of the Conference religious exhortations are filtered through pastoral reports, fiscal examinations, memorials for departed brethren, and other business involving perhaps three hundred churches. Until the World War period each preacher, as a part of the Conference, underwent a personal investigation, too. If suspected of laziness, weakness, or heresy, he was tried by an examining board. If found guilty, he surrendered his credentials and left the ministry.

A bishop presides at the Conference. But he is not necessarily the bishop of that diocese; he may be from New York or California or elsewhere, depending on what bishop is available at the moment. Because so often a strange bishop is in attendance, he has an advisory cabinet composed of the district superintendents, of which there are four or five in a normal Area. Every four years, each Conference elects delegates to a General Conference of the entire church, at which time the Discipline is revised, Bishops are elected and matters of general policy discussed.

Because the organization is loosely knit, the presiding bishop at each Conference has almost dictatorial power. He and the cabinet can send preachers to any of the three hundred churches under his jurisdiction, with or without good reason. Sometimes the bishop, on his own authority, overrides the decision of his cabinet. If Sioux City, for example, insists on a new preacher and the cabinet decides to send the minister from Charles City, the bishop may decide that the Charles City man does not have sufficient ability and select someone else. At each Conference there is a tremendous shuffling of pastorates, and many a man winds up in a charge that he does not like and that does not like him.

On the final day of Conference the bishop, amid intense excitement, adjusts his spectacles and begins a roll call. On this list is each preacher's fate for the ensuing year. He may be returned to his old town or moved. He never knows until his name is read. Sometimes he is warned that lay delegates from his church have demanded his removal. Then he is sure he will move and sends a discreet telegram to his wife at home to start packing, for the exodus to the new parsonage must take place before the following Sunday. I have seen preachers weep when the appointments were read.

Father resented this system. A little clique of powerful ministers with the bishop's ear could, and did, appropriate the important charges, leaving poor churches to less astute politicians. But father noticed early in his career that when an important church asked for a man, it usually got him.

Thus he contrived to bring about such a request when he desired to make a change. The procedure was to get the demand to the bishop long *before* Conference, for between Conferences the authority of the governing bishop of the Area is final. To be a little more explicit, Northwest Iowa falls under the jurisdiction of the Omaha Area. If a change of pastorate is required between Conferences, the bishop makes it without consulting anyone except the laymen of the churches involved. If a pastor dies, for example, his church will scout for another man, and, having found him, ask the bishop to send him at the next Conference. If a church in Omaha wants a preacher from Detroit, the Omaha bishop arranges an exchange with the bishop of the Detroit Area. Father would prevail upon the bishop to use his ad interim authority. Never once was his pastorate changed at Conference, but how he maneuvered into Fort Dodge at the age of thirty-four no one knows.

There he went, anyway, and there he remained eight years—until the thunder of his gospel became as much a part of the town as the courthouse clock. That clock was important to Fort Dodge. Each noon it struck the midday hour with a robustness heard the town over, and on the first stroke Fort Dodge set its collective watch and went home to lunch. The courthouse was across the street from the church. On his first Sunday father was in the midst of his sermon when the clock struck noon. He had to stop preaching until the clangor subsided. Meanwhile the congregation set their watches and began to fidget. For another half hour father preached—in those

days the customary sermon lasted an hour and a half—
and then pronounced the benediction. With a rush,
the body of the congregation piled out the side doors,
ignoring father at the front, in their race for home and
dinner.

Father never made that mistake again. Henceforth
his sermons were exactly twenty-four minutes long, and
his benediction was timed perfectly. The congregation
would join him in a final Amen and then stand attentively
a split second for the first stroke of the noontide bell.

This shortened service added greatly to father's
popularity. But when a church magazine gave him credit
for starting the merciful trend toward briefer pulpit
exhortation, he protested.

"Bless the clock bell, not me," he said. "On that first
Sunday I could hear stomachs rumble all over the auditorium. It is no sin to get hungry. I have never yet known
a case where a stomach committed a sin. The physical
man that transgresses is located higher up in the anatomy,
or lower down. Besides, I was hungry myself."

The courthouse was important to us for another
reason. Fort Dodge was father's first charge in a county-
seat town. Our home, being next door to the church, was
near the license bureau. Young couples coming in from
the country to be married would ask the clerk of the
court, "Where's the nearest preacher?"

Mr. McAfee, himself a Methodist, would point out
the window toward the parsonage, and the bridal couple
would rush over for the wedding. Father learned how
vital can be the perquisite of the marriage fee. Many
pairs of shoes for the children were provided by weddings,

when otherwise we might have gone barefoot to school. Father was not one to overlook this benevolence.

Many a time I was assigned to keep the watch while father was about his pastoral business. Invariably, when leaving home, he would say something like this:

"If any weddings come, I'll be at one of three places. I'm going to get some heels on these shoes, drop in at the hospital to see Mrs. Olson, and then call on Mr. Harcourt. I'll be about twenty minutes at each place."

And he would be. So when I saw a wedding coming (I can spot wedding couples to this day), I would glance at the clock, shout to mother, and race away to find father. Mother would receive the blissful couple, seat them in the parlor, and hedge until father returned, panting but benign.

Father's diligence in the pursuit of perquisites was exceeded only by mother's pinching to make the most of them. By the time father reached Fort Dodge it was impossible for us children to discover where his capability ended and mother's began.

Mother was responsible for many of father's miracles, but he never knew this, of course. If mother asked father point-blank to follow a suggestion, particularly in dealing with some church problem, he refused, distrusting any judgment except his own. So mother soon learned to use the method he himself perfected, which he proudly called his "flank attacks," getting things done indirectly.

If he wanted the official board to buy new carpeting for his study he never asked for it. He contrived to have some steward trip over an exposed surface.

In one town the parsonage basement flooded after every rain, but his appeal for repairs was ignored. After a serious illness in the family he determined to have the germ trap removed. He waited until the president of the board of trustees called. Then, beguilingly, he invited his visitor to look at the basement. Quite by accident the trustee slipped on the stairs and fell in the mud. A cement mixer was in the yard the next day.

Father delighted in these little flanking movements, all of them successful. What he never knew was that mother often played a role of her own: double-flanking *him!* Many times she would decide what had to be done and proceed obliquely to plant the seed of it in father's mind. He, pouncing finally on the idea as original with himself, then produced the attack that carried it to consummation.

Mother worked in the parish and taught a Sunday-school class. She led the devotions before the missionary societies. She played hostess to the Ladies' Aid, the Sew and So club, and the Committee for the Alleviation of the Plight of the Poor. Feminine complaints too delicate for the pastor's ear came to her, and she bolstered the sisters in all their hours of trial. She sat by sickbeds, comforted widows, consoled jilted and betrayed maidens, heard an unending stream of petty personal complaints. She was a psychiatrist before the days of psychiatry. And from her pitiful share of father's meager earnings she contributed to every charity, organized and unorganized, worthy and unworthy. All this she bore with the benignity of a Raphael Madonna.

How she did it is a mystery that no one but another minister's wife can ever understand. Many persons comment on the pious resignation of the pastor's wife and remark how lucky the preacher is to get such a perfect helpmate for his work. That's not exactly luck. Most of it is a philosophic attitude beaten into her by bitter experience with parsonages. The pastor's wife is apt to believe, after twenty years of parsonage living, that the meek were given a special blessing just for her.

When her parish work was done mother had a house to keep clean and manage, a family to cook for and keep scrubbed and mended, children to rear as community models, and a husband to comfort. She was also our buffer between father and the Methodist Discipline. She was first of all a humanitarian and second a Methodist. Loyal to father, his beliefs, and his profession and fully as mindful as he of the charges the Discipline places upon Methodist people, she nevertheless understood that frivolity is not all devilish or all amusement sinful. She could remember her own bright youth very well, and the four sisters and the brother who never thought a little mirth sinful and always enjoyed a hearty laugh, not to mention the grandmother who sometimes prescribed wine for certain illnesses. Mother was unusually pretty, too, and so youthful that even when I was in college and took her one night to a movie, one of my friends remarked, "Who was that swell girl you had a date with last night?"

The Discipline of the Methodist church is the printed collection of its rules and regulations, declarations of faith and order of services. It is amended, if need be, only by the General Conference. In the main, the Discipline sets out the tenets of the faith as handed down by John and Charles Wesley and perpetuated in America by Peter Cartwright and Francis Asbury. It also sets forth certain admonitions concerning personal conduct which are, for the most part, merely paraphrased Biblical rules of behavior. But some were taken quite literally.

For example, it was, in those days, against church rules to do any labor on the Sabbath. Mother prepared her Sunday meals on Saturday. If snow fell on Sunday the walks remained unshoveled until Monday morning. No Methodist may drink intoxicating liquor or buy or sell it. When we children were small the Discipline barred "such diversions as cannot be used in the name of the Lord Jesus," which outlawed motion pictures, the theater, and most professional entertainment. Dancing and tobacco were utterly taboo. We could not sing a song or read a book that did not "increase our knowledge of God's love." We could not play any card or other game that might be used for gambling. The church prohibited hoarding money or even the accumulation of wealth. Divorce was something to be whispered about and associated only with fallen women and Unitarians.

If these stringent church rules were rigidly enforced, the Methodists would indeed be a small society. However, only the preachers and their families are expected to abide by them. My sister and I and, later, a brother found it hard to understand why we could not play the games that the Sunday-school superintendent's children enjoyed. When we bought our first phonograph we saw no sin in a charming record called "Toddling," but father smashed it over his knee. Very often, when we children went out of bounds and violated precepts, mother glossed over our crimes and sheltered us from father's catechistic scourge. Father was the legislature that made the domestic laws, mother the police department that decided which regulations to enforce.

She never argued with us. She usually won us to obedience with tact or by an appeal to some finer trait that we possessed. She also rewarded good behavior.

In one town we lived across the street from a disagreeable woman who had a sissy son named Georgie. He angered us by bragging in front of our mothers about his music practice, his scrupulousness in making his bed and hanging up his clothes. He was the town tattletale, the kill-joy of all our amusements. There are such a mother and son in every town. One Halloween the neighbor boys decided to "fix" both mother and son. The Scott house had a great retaining wall down one side, with heavy coping stones on top. The plan was to rip off all those stones so that Georgie would have a backbreaking day's labor putting them back.

I did not enter into this sport, but I was accused of its perpetration just the same. The minister's son is first suspect in any misdemeanor. Mrs. Scott stormed our porch next morning before I was up, noisily accusing me of the nefarious business. My denials merely led her to add falsehood to my other transgressions.

Softly mother turned her away by promising that the coping stones would be replaced. Then she turned to me.

"Son," she inquired, holding up my chin so that she could look into my eyes, "did you have anything to do with this?"

"No, mother," I said with absolute truthfulness.

"Are you sure?"

"Yes, mother. Sis and I were over at the Packers' pulling taffy."

"All right," mother said, "I believe you. But Mrs. Scott is a poor widow, and she can't afford to hire a man to put back those stones. Georgie isn't strong like you, and he can't do it. You be a good boy, and as an act of Christian charity go over and fix Mrs. Scott's coping."

What could I do? The job took my whole Saturday, and I got no help from the real culprits. Strangely enough, I didn't see any of them all day.

When I returned home finally, almost at sundown, mother met me at the door.

"That was a good job," she said. "Now wash up for dinner."

When I came downstairs, my hands bruised and knicked by the heavy stones, on the dinner table was my favorite of all meals: baked beans, creamed potatoes, meat loaf. Mother smiled at me frequently.

After supper she completed my satisfaction and established me as a real hero. In her quiet voice she said, "Son, you've done your work for today. Sister and I will do the dishes."

Father had been watching this byplay and felt left out of it. He followed me onto the porch and looked across the street.

"Are you sure," he asked, chuckling, "that you had nothing to do with wrecking that coping?"

"Yes, sir," I said. I was formal with father.

"Who did?"

"I don't know, sir."

"Good boy," he grunted, and handed me a twenty· five-cent piece—probably the only money he had in his pocket.

Another time my sister had just acquired, after long saving, a mail-order ukelele and, with two neighbor children, was sitting on the front steps pecking away at it and singing popular songs. Father, who was trying to write a sermon, stormed from the house and glared down at her.

"Cut out that racket!" he commanded. "Eileen, come in the house."

The children vanished, and Eileen, weeping with humiliation, stamped into the house and smashed her ukelele on the floor. At that moment mother stepped into the hall. She went to Eileen and put an arm around her.

"You mustn't be angry with father, dear," she said. "When he is working on a sermon we must all be very quiet. He hates to write sermons as much as you hate arithmetic, and you couldn't do your algebra problems if he was playing a ukelele, could you?"

Sister, looking sorrowfully down at the wreckage, could only nod her head. She hated mathematics worse than Sunday school.

"And now," mother went on, "you have broken your ukelele just to spite yourself. That was foolish, wasn't it?"

Eileen agreed it was.

"It doesn't pay to be angry," mother concluded, as usual throwing in a moral lesson when she had a situation under control.

Again Eileen shook her head.

"All right," mother said, "you go quietly and play now. Father will have finished his sermon tomorrow and will be feeling better. Then you ask him to get you a new ukelele, and see what he says."

Mother knew very well that father was sitting in his study, searching for some way to rewin my sister's confidence without losing face. Mother figured he would be only too glad to replace the ukelele as an act of penance for his display of temper. He did, too, and it was a beauty.

We always gave right of way to father's sermons. We crept about the house like mice when he was writing them and whispered our way to bed very early on Saturday nights, that nothing would interfere with his rest before their delivery on the Sabbath. Even when we were of high school age a rigid rule was enforced that Saturday night must not for any reason be violated. Mother so carefully drummed into us the sacredness of Saturday's quiet that once when I was in serious trouble I dared not call for assistance.

I was sixteen and very much in love. Father liked the girl, too; so I never was refused the car if I was going out with Louise. One night I took her to a party, but a dashing young man who could stay out after midnight took her away from me. Badly bruised in spirit, I drove the deserted streets, dramatically sorry for myself. Very late, perhaps half-past one, I was driving up the main business street when the car hit a brick, wrenching the steering wheel from my hand.

That was too much. I jumped from the car, picked up the brick, and threw it through the biggest plate-glass window in town. Police closed in before the mighty crash had even echoed. Five minutes later I was in jail, begging the police not to disturb father's Saturday-night slumber.

But a sermon meant nothing to the law. Father answered the telephone.

"This is the police," the desk sergeant said. "You'd better come down here. We've got your son in custody."

I had the car, and so father walked. He arrived at the station a half hour later.

[41]

"What happened?" he boomed.

Tears were in my eyes. The self-pity I had been holding back all night broke in a spasm of crying.

"Louise gave me the air," I sobbed.

The stern lines in father's face softened.

"Tell me about it, son," he said gently and sat beside me.

I told the whole story.

When the narrative ended father was smiling.

"Was it a big window?" he asked.

"The biggest," the policeman said.

"Whose was it?"

"It belonged to—" and he named a member of the choir.

Father smiled broadly.

"I don't blame you a bit, son," he said. "Come along home."

We drove home together without another word, but I paid for the window from money saved working on a newspaper.

Had father been a feeble speaker we of his household might not have been so tolerant of his stern Saturday regimen. But it was not too hard to cooperate when we knew father was good. His sermons were tremendous. Children stayed voluntarily after Sunday school to hear him, proof indeed of his power. Members of the parish who had been desultory churchgoers for years developed the churchgoing habit after father came to town.

His persuasiveness had another effect, too. It raided other congregations. Baptists and Presbyterians often dropped in at our church. This led to rivalry between father and other clergymen.

In one town the Presbyterian church was across the street from our own. As father's crowds grew, Dr. Morton's diminished. Dr. Morton, who had been at his church for many years, reputedly had not written a sermon in a decade. Soon father was packing them in. Dr. Morton, conscious that his audience was shrinking but unaware of the cause, began a valiant drive to hold his flock. But by that time the damage was done. Even those who, from loyalty, went to hear him in the morning warmed our pews at night.

Finally, one winter evening, only twenty-one persons appeared in Dr. Morton's church. When it became apparent that no more were coming he stepped down to the chancel rail, saying, "There are not enough of us tonight for the usual service. So let us have an informal meeting just among ourselves instead. But I wonder what has happened? We used to be several hundred at night. Does anyone know why we now have so few?"

A guilty silence spread through the little group, and no one answered the question until, at last, a courageous soul ventured the truth.

"I think, Dr. Morton," she said, "that 'most everyone is across the street."

"Across the street?"

"Yes, hearing Mr. Spence."

Dr. Morton took the blow nobly. After an instant's sway he recovered his poise.

"In that case," he said quietly, "I think we had better join them."

And he led his congregation in single file across the street.

4

❧❧❧

THE Methodists believe in living their religion. They don't don it with their Sunday suits and hang it in moth balls the rest of the week. Methodists are church workers. Attendance on Sunday is a public showing of loyalty to the pastor and a collective revitalization of the Spirit that guides throughout the week. With so many persons of varying temperaments and ideas, all exceedingly zealous, there are bound to be jealousies and clashes of opinion over every fundamental in church and parish. Methodists often are laughed at because they are inevitably fighting about something. That is not the church's weakness but its strength.

Father pointed this out clearly one time when he refereed a particularly bitter election in the Ladies' Aid. Two women, Mrs. Cambridge, whose husband ran the town music store, and Mrs. Jellison, wife of the Maxwell auto salesman, had between them ruled the Aid society for years. They alternated in its presidency and protected each other from the job of treasurer. An agreement of long standing prevented Mrs. Cambridge from serving better refreshments when the Aid met with her than did

Mrs. Jellison, and with tacit understanding they never invited the minister's family to dinner on the same holiday.

As long as their activities remained in the church, they managed beautifully. But Mrs. Cambridge and Mrs. Jellison also were members of the Candlewick Club, which catered strictly to earthly pleasures. Eventually the day arrived when Mrs. Cambridge's daughter married. To the wedding was invited every member of Candlewick except Mrs. Jellison for the reason, as Mrs. Cambridge thought and unfortunately said, that a car salesman's wife had no business at the nuptials of a storekeeper's daughter.

Mrs. Jellison was stung. She was president that year of the Ladies' Aid, and when the annual election rolled round she refused to cooperate any longer with her late colleague. She ran for re-election. Rightly this angered Mrs. Cambridge, who couldn't see why Aid affairs had anything to do with a wedding; she certainly hadn't invited everyone in the *church* to see her daughter married. But, countered Mrs. Jellison, she *had* invited every other member of the Candlewick Club.

The controversy spread. Members of the Aid dutifully lined up on each side: the tradesmen's wives staunch for Mrs. Jellison, the merchants' wives bosom to bosom with Mrs. Cambridge. By election day the Society was divided into two snake-tongued camps, and it was obvious that, whoever won, half the society would withdraw.

Into this female maelstrom came the minister, an ex officio member of every church organization, including the Sew and So club and the Bide-a-wee Working Girls' Social club. He didn't care who won the election, but he was concerned for the Ladies' Aid. On election day he remained away until the amenities were disposed of and the women had stopped beaming at each other. Then in he came. He had a perfect right to be there, even without any knitting. Affably he chose a conspicuous front seat and began wiping his glasses with a fine linen handkerchief. Mrs. Jellison was presiding. Mrs. Cambridge was on her feet contesting the report of the nominating committee, which recommended Mrs. Jellison's re-election.

Seeing father, Mrs. Cambridge paused. That gave the chairman voice, and she looked at father.

"Do you wish to say something, Pastor?" she asked.

Father rose slowly to his feet.

"Yes," he said.

Mrs. Cambridge fell back among her smoldering henchwomen. From Mrs. Jellison's side of the aisle arose another buzz, but with an entirely different inflection.

"I understand," father began pleasantly, "that you good women are having a fight. I never missed a fight in my life except once—I was laid up with the measles."

The Jellison contingent smiled. Mrs. Cambridge led her faction in an icy stare.

The preacher looked at the presiding chair, then at Mrs. Cambridge.

"I came," he went on, "because I knew this would be a capital scrap. I have seen you women battling for the Lord shoulder to shoulder so often that I wanted to see what you are like toe to toe."

His infectious smile won a few converts in a neutral corner.

"I like a good fight," he said. "The Bible is full of battles. But the wars that were successful were those the

Children of Israel fought *together* against a common foe. It wasn't until they began fighting among themselves that they were conquered."

He let that sink in. No one was smiling now.

"If I entered a church and found everyone in harmony I'd know something was wrong. Over the years I have learned to judge a new charge by the number of fights in progress among the membership. Fighting is proof of activity, and activity is a sign of health. Show me a fighting church and I'll show you a church that is getting the Lord's work done."

He paused, inviting comment. But there was none.

"It is the same in your society," he went on. "You are doing a great work for this church. I would hate to see that work interrupted. You good sisters have enough on your hands fighting for the new hymnals. I suggest you reject the report of your nominating committee and entertain nominations for the presidency from the floor."

As he said this he looked at Mrs. Brooks, a farmer's wife who would backstop her preacher in anything. She jumped up.

"I so move," she called.

It was done. Mrs. Jellison and Mrs. Cambridge were furious, but prudent. Another quick look and a second loyal sister was on her feet, nominating an outsider who had not participated in the feud. Father glanced again at Mrs. Brooks.

"I move that the nominations be closed," she piped swiftly. A few voted "aye," but none dared voice a "nay."

Father walked from the meeting, knowing what would follow. Mrs. Jellison would invite Mrs. Cambridge to dinner. Mrs. Cambridge would accept. The women would put their heads together to prevent control of the society from slipping permanently from their hands.

When father returned home mother opened the door for him. She had avoided attending the meeting to escape the controversy, but she was anxious.

"How did it go?" she asked.

"Perfectly. They'll be cussing me out of Christendom tonight, but they'll be sitting together in church next Sunday."

And they were.

Sometimes an issue developed over a matter that touched collective personal prejudices and proved too fundamental to be handled, as was the Ladies' Aid election, by a quick flank attack. Prejudices caused father his most anxious moments. But if he decided a matter of principle was involved he would defy the entire congregation.

The minister who had preceded father at Fort Dodge was a Southerner. How he had arrived in a Northern church was one of the peculiar mysteries of church politics. During Dr. Caldwell's pastorate a prejudice against Negroes filtered through the congregation until the members would not even employ a Negro sexton.

Father was aware of this, but he knew that a dutiful blast from the pulpit would only intensify the feeling. So he became a personal example of kindliness toward the few Negroes in town. He helped the African M.E. preacher with a revival meeting and called him "Brother" on the street. A few parishioners talked, but not many.

Then one spring day a Negro musician came to town

for a recital. "Blind Henry," they called him. A fine pianist, his particular act of showmanship was to invite the town's best music teacher to the platform to play any number she desired. He would play it after her. This gave a local musician a chance to shine and was easy for Blind Henry. Almost every small-town musician, showing off her best work, plays Chopin. Henry knew Chopin by heart.

Blind Henry was to play in our church because it was the town's largest auditorium. My sister at that time was studying the piano. When father told Blind Henry that Eileen would be unable to hear him because of illness, the musician went to the parsonage to play for her. We were so absorbed in listening that we did not notice Eileen's schoolteacher approach to learn why she had not attended school. Miss Millrose, peering through a porch window, saw Eileen not only out of bed but listening respectfully to a Negro being entertained in the pastor's home.

Miss Millrose did not even knock. Back to school she went and, after weeks of petty persecution, failed my sister.

When Eileen brought home her report card, father was so upset he was able to eat only one portion of Swiss steak at dinner. For the first time he, as a preacher, had been attacked through his children, and the unfairness of such tactics enraged him. He walked the floor between his study and the front porch for an hour after dinner, then sought mother.

"All right," he pronounced with the finality of a last judgment, "all right. I'll show them—every mother's son of them!"

[49]

Then began an amazing summer. One Sunday morning the congregation found its choir absent; in its place, a traveling troupe from the Piney Woods school was singing spirituals. Another Sunday a Negro bishop from the South was guest preacher. On still other days father exchanged pulpits with Brother Hankins of the African church—all this without a word of explanation.

As the teacher of the men's Bible class remarked one morning, "We come to church to learn right from wrong, but now we can scarcely tell black from white."

A dutiful parishioner repeated the remark to father at the close of service that very day.

"That's fine," father replied quickly. "If Brother Wilson is amused, he can't be very badly upset."

Quietly an argument germinated and spread through the congregation. Those with the dearest memories of Dr. Caldwell, father's predecessor, those who had held church offices under him and now had none, became vocally anti-Negro. Father's friends and church appointees, the farm contingent that is always loyal, and those to whom he had ministered in joy and sorrow lined up behind him.

As the time of school reopening arrived, with the Annual Conference only four weeks away, the fight broke into the open. The first blast came at the fourth Quarterly Conference, which decides whether the preacher shall be invited back for another year. Major Charles Wainwright Cooper, who had fought for the Confederacy and never let anyone forget it, arose at the invitation to new business. The district superintendent was presiding.

"Am I to understand," the major began, challenging father, "that you asked the school superintendent to advance your daughter from the third to fourth grade, although she failed to pass last spring?"

Father's jaw squared.

"I did," he admitted.

"Am I to understand," the major went on, "that you raised the accusation of race prejudice against the teacher who did not pass your child?"

"I did."

"May I inquire the circumstances?"

"You may."

The room was very quiet. This was strictly a private fight. Nobody wanted to get mixed up in it. Members knew from experience that their preacher could not be beaten in face-to-face debate.

"Miss Millrose," father commenced, with the peculiar little sigh that always escaped him when he was fighting to inhibit a show of anger, "told three sisters of this church that my daughter Eileen was as bright as any third-grade child and that Eileen was failed to show the pastor of this church that he could not fraternize with colored people."

"Is it true," the inquisitor pursued, "that you demanded Miss Millrose's resignation?"

"It is not true. I distinctly told Brother Haynes (the school superintendent) that if Miss Millrose would be at all embarrassed I would drop the whole matter and send my daughter to the parochial school."

That was a blast. Father had counted on it to break Major Cooper's attack. He was not disappointed. Half a dozen members leaped up, exclaiming simultaneously, "You did what?" while others looked around apprehensively as if expecting the church to cave in.

Calmly father repeated his remark. The tumult increased, until the district superintendent's voice cut across the babel.

"Silence, brethren!" he shouted. "Give Brother Spence a chance to explain."

Father walked firmly to the front of the room and turned to face everyone.

"In the parochial school," he said, "they do not teach racial intolerance. It is written, 'Love thy neighbor as thyself.' The gospel of Christ is the lesson I want my children to learn, and I will send them where it is taught. It would be a shame if a Methodist child had to learn to be a good Methodist from the Catholics because of bigotry in her own church. Tolerance, brethren, is something we might all learn from the Sisters of Charity."

He left the meeting then, knowing that a terrific debate would follow over the question whether to invite him to return for another year. Anxiously he walked the floor at home. Finally the telephone rang.

"Well, Brother Spence," the district superintendent reported, "you won, but you'd better be careful. The minority faction will take this to Conference."

"I'll be ready," father said, his face ashen.

The next morning, while walking downtown, he met Father Murphy.

"I understand," the priest baited him gently, "that you had need to summon our assistance last night."

"Father Murphy," the Methodist minister said, smiling graciously, "I'd call on the Devil in Hell if he would be of any help. But I figured invoking your assistance would be preferable."

This conversation was overheard by two Methodists

and a freethinker who stood outside a bookstore, await-
ing delivery of the Chicago papers. By noon the story
was all over town, and father's stock began to go up. He
might even have warded off the attack at Conference
except for an untoward incident that occurred the
following week.

A celebrated Negro singer came to town. Father never
overlooked the chance to hear a great musician practice
and was always discreetly in the background when an
artist tested the acoustics of the church auditorium,
where important town concerts were always held.

After the practice father walked forward and introduced himself.

"I wish," he remarked, "that I had a voice like yours
in my choir."

"Thank you, sir," the singer said respectfully.
"Perhaps you can help me. You see—my wife and I
can't eat in the restaurant here, and we were turned
away at the hotel. I wonder if you have a little room
where we may rest until the recital."

Father gasped.

"You come right over to the house," he said. "We
have a spare room. And, of course, you'll have dinner
with us."

The Negro and his wife remained overnight. By noon
next day the anti-Negro group was organizing the parish
again.

5

꩜

WHEN father heard that the Negro issue had been revived, he hunted up mother. He found her busy with the morning house cleaning.

"Do you suppose," he asked, following her into the bathroom, "that those stupid fools really will take this to Conference?"

"I guess they will," mother murmured, picking up the soiled towels and putting them in a hamper.

"But they haven't a leg to stand on," father protested, looking around for a place to put the scrubbing pail she had handed him. "They can't ask me to move just because I want them to be tolerant."

Mother wiped the washbowl with her cloth. "They might make something, though," she said quietly, "of your threat to send Eileen to a Catholic school."

"Ah, bosh," father snorted, setting the pail down where mother would trip over it. "That was just a meeting buster. Nobody took it seriously."

Patiently mother picked up the pail and stood back to put fresh towels on the rack.

"The bishop might," she suggested.

"H-m-m-m," said father, following her into the hall and unconsciously handing her a dust mop from the closet. With hands tucked under his suspenders, he pursued her. "I can fix that. I'll find a precedent for it in the bishop's ministry in China."

He chuckled, took the dust mop, and returned it to the closet.

"What if the men don't apply a specific accusation," mother suggested, "but just ask for your removal?" She walked into Eileen's room and began to make the bed.

"That's a horse of another color," said father, blocking the doorway.

"Yes, it is," mother agreed.

"You don't suppose they'd really do that, do you?" he worried. "They'd want a sure case. Too many people are loyal to me here. I could organize a counter-demonstration that would shiver the bishop's spine."

He trudged down the backstairs behind mother and into the kitchen, where he leaned against the wall while she attacked the morning dishes.

"That," she objected, "would be proof that you needed to fight."

"H-m-m-m," murmured father, "so it would."

He was silent, now, but not for long.

"I wish I hadn't said that about the Catholics."

Mother let him wrestle with that one by himself. She did her housework quickly, without waste motion. Occasionally she handed him a stack of dishes to put away. Dutifully he did so, without being aware of it. Mother got a great deal of work out of him when he was thinking about something else.

[55]

"Don't you think what I said to Father Murphy on the street will scotch this Catholic business?"

"No," said mother, giving him a dish towel to hang up, "I think just the opposite."

"Why?"

He had to pursue her into the living room to hear the answer.

"Because you put the church laundry on the front line for the whole town to see. People will resent that."

"But only a few," father argued, busy now slapping a dustcloth over chairs and sofa.

"It only takes one," mother reminded him, improving on the dusting with quick flicks of her own, "especially if that one seeks help."

"From whom?"

Mother pretended to be dusting the piano.

"Oh, from other pastors, perhaps."

Father dropped suddenly into his leather chair.

"That's possible," he said.

"Suppose," mother went on, "that Major Cooper organizes a few of the pastors who were angry last year because you came to Fort Dodge and they accuse you of something specific?"

"Such as —?"

"Well —" mother went to work on the bookcases, sure that father was listening carefully, "in view of your praise of the Catholics, they might ask you to stand trial on charges on heresy."

Father leaped up.

"They'd never dare!"

He watched mother disappear into the library and then went after her.

"What *would* they do?" she asked.

"They'd —" he held out his hand for the dustcloth again, "they'd probably cook up something."

Mother assumed particular industry.

"Suppose," she ventured, "they asked you to preach the Conference sermon and then riddled it with holes? You know any sermon can be challenged if isolated sentences are used for examples."

"H-m-m-m," said father, getting in her way before the folding doors separating library from parlor could come between them.

Mother trudged upstairs to her bedroom and sat down with her darning. Father tagged along.

"You know," he said, "I'd rather have something like that to fight—something I could get my teeth in—than be kicked out without any charges."

"I know you would, dear," mother answered, her needle attacking an enormous hole in her son's stocking.

Father began walking up and down. As his mind took hold of the problem the length of his stride increased. Finally he paused altogether, and a twinkle came into his eye.

"How's this," he beamed. "I will get old George Settles off in a corner and tell him, man to man, that the only thing I'm afraid of is that they'll get help from some other preachers and accuse me of heresy—that I can beat anything else into the ground. I'll tell him I'm only confiding in him because I have to tell somebody or bust wide open, and I know I can trust him. He'll go straight to Cooper as fast as he can hitch a horse, and, mark my words, by sundown Major Cooper will be on his way to

Sioux City with as neat a scheme as anybody ever hatched."

Mother nodded proudly. Her strategy had worked. "That's fine, dear," she encouraged him. "But what will you do then?"

"Oh, don't worry about that," father said, and a moment later the front door slammed behind him. Mother, needle idle now, watched him through a window as he strode confidently down the street in the general direction of George Settles' pickle works.

When father returned dinner was nearly ready. Since he had not been home to lunch mother assumed he had been successful. She handed him a bundle of silver with which to set the table.

"Tell me about it," she invited.

"Mr. Settles was easy. After I took him into my confidence, I went over to the bank. Through the window I watched him go over to the courthouse and chat with Major Cooper, who was sitting on his usual bench on the lawn. The major went home immediately. Then I lunched with Dr. Romer, just to be sure that most of our delegates will be on my side. Finally, the major caught the five-thirty train for Sioux City. Undoubtedly he's on his way to see Stillman and a few other preachers. From the heft of his bag I'd say he was planning to be gone a week."

"He didn't see you!" mother exclaimed.

"He sure did," father chuckled. "I was down at the station, paying a pastoral call on the ticket agent when he showed up. He turned five shades of green when he saw me and mumbled something about going up to the city to sell some cattle."

"What did you say to that?" mother asked, holding her breath.

"I said," father laughed, slapping his knee, "that I hoped he'd get what he wanted."

Two days later father received a telegram from Bishop S——. "Want you preach Conference Sunday sermon," it read, "please reply."

Father found mother in the basement ironing and put the telegram on her board.

"Well," he announced, "here it is."

"They're working fast," mother said, dexterously smoothing a starched collar. Father always had at least fourteen shirts in the weekly wash.

"That's the way Stillman works," father grunted. "You remember how quickly he organized, trying to get Fort Dodge for himself last year. I'll bet a hat he took Major Cooper's bait—hook, line, and sinker."

Mother toyed with the dampened clothes, looking for something easy. She selected a pile of handkerchiefs and went to work.

"What sermon will you preach?"

Father pondered. "How about that one from Daniel: 'O King, I have done no hurt'?"

"No," mother objected quickly, "that would put you on the defensive."

"So it would," father agreed, beginning a tiger pace from the washtubs to the ash pile to the fruit cellar and back again.

"How about that humdinger from Ephesians: 'Put on the whole armor of God'? Maybe by implication they would get the rest of the quotation —"

Mother picked up the verse where father had dropped

[59]

it. "'That ye may be able to stand against the wiles of the devil. . . . ' No, that would only antagonize them."

"How about a missionary sermon? Nobody could find fault with that, especially since benevolences haven't come in very well this year."

Mother selected some table linen from her basket and continued ironing. "No, it must be something special for the occasion."

Father gazed at the labels on a shelf of jelly jars, then wheeled back to the washtub.

"How about building a sermon on Paul's letter to the Corinthians? 'It is a very small thing that I should be judged of you . . . for I know nothing against myself.'"

"That's not subtle."

"No," father admitted, star... into the ashpit, "but it would make a whale of a sermon. Remind me to order some more coal."

Mother put aside her iron.

"Haven't you a book of Bishop S——'s sermons?"

"Yes," said father, "*The Cathedral of Pines*, I think it is."

"Why don't you go up and read the bishop's sermons? They might give you an idea."

Father stopped meandering.

"What do you mean?" he asked.

"Well," said mother innocently, "if you are going to be on trial you should be particularly careful not to preach anything which violates the bishop's own theology. You wouldn't want him against you."

Father thought that over.

"All right," he assented, "but I don't see what good it will do."

He stomped upstairs and remained in the library until dinnertime. Then, when we were seated, he emerged and said grace with all the confidence of the redeemed. The sparkle had returned to his eyes.

"Well?" asked mother anxiously, as he began to carve the beef roast.

"I have a plan," he said.

6

⟨﹏⟩

THE week before Conference father was a bear. Not only had he to collect all financial arrears and check the annual reports of societies and organizations but he had his Conference sermon to prepare.

He would retire to his study immediately after breakfast. For several hours we would hear him pace up and down, talking to himself. Occasionally a book slammed on his desk. Now and again he kicked the hot-air register with a comforting bang. Then he would emerge, his face tense, and slam out of the house for a long walk in the courthouse grounds. This went on intermittently all week.

Finally the day came for him to leave for Cherokee, where the Conference was to be held. The lay delegates, only two of whom were in league with Major Cooper, had already gone on.

Mother walked with father halfway to the station, talking to him earnestly.

"Now remember, dear," she said in parting, "not a

word to anybody. Don't let your habit of talking get hold of you. You don't know who your friends are."

He leaned down and kissed her.

"God bless you," he said. "If the house burns, get the kids and the sermons. Let the rest go. If we have to move I'll send you a wire."

"Oh, send me one anyway," she called after him, with a final show of bravery, "I so seldom get a telegram."

The days passed with aching slowness, the monotony broken only by short letters from Cherokee that increased rather than eased the anxiety.

"Stillman has things well organized," father wrote. "He sees his chance to get into Fort Dodge and is pursuing it with more diligence than ever he chased a sinner. The major is here, of course. Though not a delegate, he explains his presence by saying he came for spiritual guidance. I think he'll get it."

Next day another letter came:

"The bishop took me aside and warned that the brethren will challenge my sermon after the service Sunday. I am sure he is on my side. He told me that once in Hankow, when the bandits came, he took his whole flock for refuge into the Catholic mission because it had a high wall. 'The wall,' he said, 'was really to keep us Methodists out, but I just told the good Jesuit father that we had been battering so long at the walls of Heaven it was no trick at all to break into his cloister.' "

On Friday:

"The report from our parish is the best in the entire Conference. If the good brethren were hunting for a weakness in my armor here, they are very disappointed. Also, I noticed Mrs. Baker and a half dozen other mem-

[63]

bers take the bishop aside. We have some very loyal
friends, mother, and they are coming to our rescue, for
which God be thanked."

Then Saturday:

"Pray for me tonight and tomorrow, for I shall need
you."

When mother read that letter, she summoned my
sister and me and bade us bathe in a hurry. Father was in
real trouble, and she was going to be with him.

We slipped into Cherokee and went to the Methodist
parsonage, where we spent the night. We didn't see
father until Sunday morning, when he stepped into the
pulpit with the bishop and four district superintendents.
We were inconspicuously seated in the balcony and did
nothing to attract his attention, but father spotted us
during the organ prelude. His eyes brightened, and he
started to smile, then quickly rubbed his nose to conceal
his curving lips. Then he crossed his knees and began to
bob a leg up and down, a sure sign that he was pleased.

As though this were a regular Sunday, the service
started. There was nothing unusual about its beginning
except that, after the Cherokee pastor had read out the
hymns, the choir yelled a little louder and longer than
usual for the benefit of the visiting bishop. A district
superintendent led the prayer. Another superintendent
read from the Psalter. Then the bishop quoted the Scripture and made almost endless announcements. A third
superintendent exhorted the congregation to be liberal
and started the collection plates on their way. Again the
choir sang, as badly as before.

Then father arose, dressed in his best: winged collar
and ascot, black vest with white starched piqué facing,

Prince Albert coat, and striped trousers. He was an amazing figure, but far more impressive than his habiliments were the angle of his jaw, the glint in his eye, and the softening aura of devoutness contributed by the gentle blue light that came, like a blessing, through a stained-glass window.

Father looked over the congregation serenely, estimating to within ten or a score the number of persons present. Then he took out his watch, detached it from its chain, and set it on the pulpit. Calmly he opened his Bible, read a text, laid the Book down, stepped a little to one side of the pulpit in full view of everyone, particularly the three hundred visiting ministers, and began to preach.

He used no notes, but spoke from memory. His words articulated to the rafters, though they were softly pitched. After the first few sentences he glanced at the bishop, and an impish flash crossed between them. The sermon he preached was a great one. There was no doubt of it in the mind of anyone present.

When it ended there was a hush of respect. The bishop rose and pronounced the benediction. Most of the congregation sauntered out, taking endless time, while the preachers pretended to be talking to one another or perused the notes they had made furtively during the sermon. Finally, when only the pastors and a few interested laymen remained, the Reverend Mr. Stillman rose to his feet to address the chair.

"If it please the bishop," he called out, "I ask that a business meeting be convened at once to deliberate a matter that cannot wait until tomorrow."

The bishop's gavel fell. The preachers tensed in their pews. The dread charge of heresy was about to be levied.

A board of trial examiners would be appointed in order to present a damning report on the morrow just before the Conference adjourned. Mother gripped our hands, and her eyes fixed themselves on father with a gaze that did not waver except once, when father deliberately winked at her.

"There has been much talk," Stillman went on, "concerning the ecclesiastical heresy of one of our brethren."

He let that sink in deeply.

"I would be exceedingly reluctant to bring such a charge against a brother without the most careful foundation," he continued, "for, once made, such a charge cannot easily be withdrawn and must of necessity receive right of way until prov~ ~ ~~ or false."

He paused, as though his task was painful.

"You have a charge," the bishop asked in his routine voice, "to prefer against a brother?"

"I have."

"Will you name it?"

Another preacher intervened.

"May it please the bishop," he asked, "that I be heard?"

The bishop nodded. "If the brother who has the floor will yield."

Stillman sank from the spotlight, and the plan so carefully laid out in corridors and hotel rooms began to unfold, sometimes almost buried in polite words and parliamentary routine.

As the sparring continued, father's leg bobbed up and down, and his lips and eyes threatened to break into a smile. He spotted a few of his parishioners in the church: Major Cooper and Mr. Settles on the attackers' side;

Mrs. Baker, who could ill afford the journey, sitting quietly beside Dr. Romer and his wife.

Every time Mrs. Baker's eyes met the major's, the old war horse retired from the field. Many more were there, winking encouragement to the pastor's family up above or guiltily staring at the floor.

For half an hour caution prevailed, then Stillman took the floor again.

"You have heard," he said, preparing now to mention father's name, "how one of our number advocated in open meeting the training of Methodist youth in Catholic schools. This in itself, while worthy of rebuke, is not enough to bring upon his head a serious charge. For that we must look farther afield." Stillman adjusted his glasses and picked up the notes he had made during the sermon. "I would like to make reference to the sermon we have heard this morning."

The bishop appeared to be choking. Father's leg pumped more excitedly.

"The third chapter of Mark, from which our text this morning was taken, truly says: 'For whosoever shall do the will of God, the same is my brother.' That is a noble text. But there is another admonition in that chapter which Brother Spence seemingly has forgotten. Let us refresh his memory: 'Whosoever shall blaspheme against the Holy Spirit hath never forgiveness, but is guilty of an eternal sin.'

"Now let you one and all be judge whether an eternal sin has been committed here this morning. Our brother told an anecdote which happened to our church in China. With gripping reality he described how the coolie, starving during the great famine, went into the church and, from tne altar of God, stole the rice which had been laid there as an offering and took it home to his family. With copious tears our brother says—I read his very words: 'Was that a sin? To steal from the altar of God to feed his children? I think not.' "

Stillman pointed around the auditorium. "Mark that well, brethren," he cried. "He said: '*I* think not.' He set himself up as judge of what, in the eyes of the Lord, shall be called a sin. The Bible says: 'Judge not that ye be not judged.' The Bible also says: 'Thou shalt not steal.' The crime depicted was a double one: stealing from the very font of God, the church. By what right does our brother cloak himself in the mantle of the Holy Spirit and judge his fellow men? Has he taken unto himself the power of judgment reserved for the Holy Trinity? I shudder at the implications which must be in the minds of all of you. I could say more, but this is enough."

The cudgel passed quickly to another and yet another. Several quotations from the sermon were dissected, drawn, quartered, and damned. Then father's defenders sprang up, the church rang with oratory, and all the while the bishop's complexion grew redder and redder.

Finally father could stand it no longer. Rising deliberately, he stepped to the pulpit, picked up a little gray book, opened it conspicuously at a center page, and handed it to the nearest district superintendent.

That brother looked at the title, read a few lines, opened his mouth in amazement, and quickly passed the book to the colleague on his right. He, too, read, reeled, and passed the book along. Father and the bishop tried hard not to watch. But the assembled ministers saw and grew curious.

Dr. Benesh, the district superintendent who had led the offertory prayer, hurriedly descended from the pulpit and placed the volume in the hands of a conspirator.

That brother read, reread, and almost strangled. Then he hastened to Mr. Stillman, who was rising to his feet to make the fatal charge. Stillman frowned with annoyance at the interruption and waved the book away. But his friend insisted, whispering audibly. Impatiently Stillman

[69]

took the book and gestured to throw it aside until his eye caught the title. He turned to the appointed page and read, then weakly sat down.

The stillness of a sacrament now hushed the church.

Ponderously the bishop rose to his feet.

"If there is a charge to be made against a brother," he said solemnly, "let it be made now. There has been debate enough."

Not a word was uttered anywhere in the great church.

"None appearing," the bishop continued, "I will proceed to close. But before I do, I would like to add one remark to what has been said. In the third chapter of Mark there is still another useful text. You will find it in the twenty-fourth and twenty-fifth verses. 'And if a kingdom be divided against itself, that kingdom shall not be able to stand. And if a house be divided against itself, that house will not be able to stand.'"

The bishop's bushy eyebrows turned down into a pontifical frown.

"I charge every man here," he roared, "as the first duty of his new pastoral year, to go home from this Conference and write a sermon on that text. Let it be preached in every church in this Conference on Sunday morning next."

The preachers departed quietly. Mr. Stillman remained, head bowed over the little gray book, reading the bishop's sermon that father had delivered to the Conference word for word.

7

✦

WHEN a preacher returns to a charge for a new year
after a minority has fought to oust him, he must be exceedingly careful not to be vindictive against his op-
ponents. One sharp word, one manifestation of bitterness,
and his usefulness would be at an end. Scrupulously he
must turn the other cheek. He must forgive and forget and
by example alone prove the opposition wrong.

Father knew this well, and, on the train en route home
from Cherokee for another year at Fort Dodge, was careful to point out to my sister and me the necessity for tact
on our part, too.

"You must forget everything that has happened," he
told us. "Just pretend we are moving to a new church. Be
as nice to Mr. Settles and Major Cooper as you can be.
And, above all, don't thank the people who defended us."

When the train stopped father stepped from the day
coach in full dignity. Mother followed, careful to let no
more than the tip of a toe show beneath her skirt.

No welcoming committee greeted us, however. The
only church member present was the town liveryman,
who leaped from his box and approached his pastor.

"Good morning, Naboth," father called out with a smile. "A beautiful day."

"Yes, sir," Naboth replied, "and a good day for you to be coming back to us, sir."

"Any other passengers?" father asked. He looked around, but the platform was deserted.

"No, sir," Naboth answered spryly, "just yourselves. Get in now, before Maud gets rambunctious."

But father hesitated. "We're paying for our ride this time, Naboth."

"No charge for the preacher," Naboth retorted. "Why, even the horse wouldn't tolerate it, would you, Maud?"

"Then we'll walk," father announced. "You can't always be driving us for nothing, Naboth. I'd rather pay you honestly and see your envelope a little fatter in the collection plate."

"You don't need to worry about that, either. Corinne and I decided to give ten dollars more this year. We—" Naboth suddenly became busy with mother's handbag, "we're busier now, so we can afford a little more. And— well, we just feel it is worth a little more to have you back, sir. We was pretty well broken up when we heard—"

"That's all right, Naboth," father cut in gently. "You can afford *twenty* dollars more, you old skinflint. Didn't you trade that spavined mare for a gaited gelding and sell him to Dr. Harlow for $200?"

Naboth eased mother's bag onto the box and looked stealthily over his shoulder. "Now, who ever said such a thing?" he asked.

" 'The walls have a thousand ears,' " father quoted, "and besides, I was talking to Peter Harper up at—"

"You know, parson," Naboth interrupted quickly, "those curls on your little daughter are getting longer and prettier every day."

"Don't compliment the child," father said, handing mother into the rig. "She's vain enough already. And don't think you can confuse the issue by flattery. We pay for this ride."

"No, Reverend," the liveryman countered, "I can't take money from my pastor. You didn't ask me for anything when you sat up all night with my baby the night she died. And besides, Doc Romer didn't charge you for taking out the children's tonsils, and if he can be generous so can I."

"Be generous with the Lord, Naboth," father said, "and give His servants enough that they, too, can be generous. I'll pay my way."

By now everything except a large box was loaded.

"That yours?" Naboth asked, pointing to the crate.

"Yes," father admitted, glancing guiltily at mother. "Some new books I bought at Conference. I hope they will help me preach better sermons."

"We ain't complaining," Naboth said. "I tell you what I'll do. You can't pay for your ride, but I'll charge you fifty cents' drayage on them books. All right?"

"All right," father chuckled. "Some day I'll learn not to argue with a horse trader."

Naboth clucked Maud to a trot, and we started the fourteen-block ride home. We rounded the Square, where on Saturdays farmers hitched their rigs and on summer evenings there were concerts by the Volunteer Firemen's band. Just then Seth Winegartner, "purveyor of table delicacies deluxe imported in 48 hours by fast freight from Chicago!" stepped through the doors of his grocery.

"Good morning, Mr. Spence," he called. "Very glad to see you with us again, sir."

Father waved back, noticing as he did so that in the window was a new vegetable cooler: a series of bright-green metal trays over which water sprayed, keeping the lettuce crisp and the carrots bright.

"That new freshener looks mighty fine," he said.

On we went into Main Street, clopping over the cobblestones. At the Harmony Music House, James Cambridge waved both hands, and we all answered his welcome.

"We'll be ordering that new piano, now," father advised the merchant. "Is that A. B. Chase still on the floor?"

"Indeed it is, Mr. Spence," Cambridge replied. "I gave it an extra coat of polish this morning."

Slowly the carriage proceeded, pulling wide around the hardware store, where a half dozen farmers' buggies were tied. The merchant saw us and came to the door.

"Mighty glad you'll be back, Brother Spence."

"Thanks, Brother Wilson."

Father nodded to right and left as we went on down a straight line between two rows of three-story business blocks. Occasionally a carriage passed, and its occupants exchanged salutations with us. Other greetings broke from the curb. Father, in answer, addressed everyone by name and two by nicknames: Hunk, the shoe shiner at Hodges' Pharmacy, and Dick, the porter at the barbershop. Then Maud rounded the corner of Third Avenue North, kicked up her heels a little for the drummers on the long wooden porch of the Wakonsa Hotel, and we were home.

Father looked up proudly at the tall steeple of his own church, which cast a shadow on the courthouse. "When the sun is in the southeast," he said, "I'm afraid there is almost too much union between church and state. When we build a new church we'll put the steeple on the other street."

Naboth swung around. "New church?" he gasped.

"Just an idea for the future, Naboth," father replied quickly. "People as fine as our membership deserve a nobler edifice."

With boyish enthusiasm he jumped from the carriage and lifted first mother and then us to the stepping block.

"Welcome home, my dears," he said.

All afternoon the parsonage door remained open while members of the church passed in and out. The first arrival was Mrs. Settles, laden with a basket of her husband's best pickle products. Father received her graciously as an ambassador of peace, stating candidly that he held no resentment against her husband. Father always took particular pains to be obvious with Mrs. Settles; otherwise she misunderstood and misinterpreted everything he did or said.

As she left the McGregor and Albertson families arrived. Before meeting the newcomers father had time to whisper, "Mark my words, mother, we'll be invited to the Settles' house for Sunday dinner." Then he rushed to the door to steer all the four McGregor daughters away from two weak-legged parlor chairs. Such diplomacy was necessary, for the McGregor girls were six feet tall. Father delighted in calling them the "daughters of Anak."

"Come in, come in," he invited brightly, flicking a finger at Eileen and me to sit quickly in the Tudor chairs. "What on earth have you got in that basket?"

"Brother Spence," said Rachel, who stacked cordwood in her father's woodyard, "we were so tickled yesterday when we saw in the paper that you were coming back that we spent last night making you some candy. Here are all your favorites."

The sisters produced a huge basket bedecked with a red ribbon. They were wonderful cooks, and father knew what they had brought: a layer of divinity that would melt in his mouth, leaving soft black walnuts; a layer of panocha, generous with hazelnuts; a big corner packed with stuffed dates; another corner of cream-soft fudge, each square garnished with a whole walnut, and, tucked down at the bottom, a few creamed filberts that no one else in town could make.

Neither the McGregors nor the Albertsons were "quality folk" (merchants), like the Cambridge and Wilson families, or processors like the Settleses, or manufacturers like Foerster Ross. They were artisans and tradesmen, as were those who made up the bulk of the congregation. They were the people who, despite many human shortcomings, worked hard and loyally for their church—the parishioners whose contributions entailed the greatest sacrifice. And they were the ones with whom father felt most at home and for whom he often arose in the depth of a winter night when they were in physical or spiritual pain; they, the needy to whom Dr. Romer referred when he said, "They call the parson first and me second."

All afternoon they arrived—the Baileys, the Dorsets, the Smiths, and the Jones, in a festive procession—and it was almost seven o'clock when the last guest departed, permitting us to relax at last. For several minutes we sat quietly rallying our strength; then the telephone summoned father.

"I was right, mother," he said, as he hung up the receiver. "Mrs. Settles invited us to Sunday dinner, and I accepted."

"I wish," mother replied wearily, "she had made it tonight. I'll go and see what I can find for supper."

She was just starting for the kitchen when a great "whoa" sounded at the front curb. From a handsome rubber-tired buggy tumbled three couples: the Brookses, the Shannons, and the Wellmans, from Shady Springs Road.

They entered with such merry shouts and cheers of welcome that Veronica O'Connor, the saloonkeeper's daughter next door, peeped from behind her lace curtains to see the fun.

Bringing up the rear came Farmer Brooks, mighty uncomfortable in his store suit. Up the steps he carried a crate of apples, the first pick from his twenty-acre Jonathan orchard.

"We're a mite late," he boomed, "but we don't come empty-handed."

Into the parlor, which was reserved exclusively for receptions and weddings, came the box of apples.

The Shannons had brought a fat goose, stuffed with chestnuts and already roasted. The Wellmans, who were tenant farmers, produced a loin of salt pork.

Quickly mother took the farm women into the kitchen, where they would feel at home, and as their husbands talked and slapped their preacher on the back the women went to work on a supper that a threshing crew would have admired. Coffee was boiled, the goose was heated,

[77]

its grease was ladled into a jar against the children's winter croup, and a few apples became a pie. Eileen and I stood by helplessly, trying to cooperate and merely getting underfoot.

By the time Farmer Brooks had summarized the results of his summer's work and Farmer Wellman had praised his landlord (without too great a show of enthusiasm) the repast was on the table.

Father flashed his carving knife and folded back the goose with the skill of a surgeon. He waited calmly until conversation ebbed, then pronounced a brief blessing, and began to serve.

"He carves wonderfully," shouted Mrs. Shannon, well satisfied with her generous helping of breast and dressing. "I wish Charlie would take a few lessons."

Mother smiled.

"It's always a game with Will," she said, "to see if he can get everybody served before the first plate gets cold."

Wellman, whose napkin was tucked under his chin, added hungrily, "He's going to do it, too, by gum."

The party broke up at nine, for even behind the Brookses' fast bays six miles was a long ride home at night. Father and mother went with them to the stoop.

"We'll see you Sunday if it don't rain," the Wellmans said. And this was no witticism. Iowa farm roads, A.D. 1910, were quagmires during the spring and autumn rains.

Father and mother waved them on their way. Seeing the street deserted, father kissed mother quickly.

"They're wonderful people," mother exclaimed.

"Yes," father affirmed, "of such is the Kingdom of Heaven."

8

❧✣❧

$\mathcal{S}$ UNDAY morning in a preacher's household belongs to the head of the house. Everybody makes way for the pastor. The children tiptoe lest they disturb their father's last-minute meditations. And a schedule is imposed so that the bathroom will be free and the house quiet when the minister dresses for his morning service.

In our house an unerring routine was followed. But on the first Sunday after his heresy trial father arose at six instead of seven and retired to his study for an extra hour of prayer.

By half-past seven the coffeepot was off the stove, and four glasses of orange juice stood on the kitchen table.

"Son," mother called softly up the back stairs, "you may get the oatmeal now."

Sleepily I tumbled from bed and grumbled my way to the basement. I was very young, but not too young for my Sunday duties to be well established. From a fireless cooker in the fruit cellar I lifted a pot of oatmeal and carried it upstairs. That cooker was a wonderful blessing to us, for a warm breakfast could be prepared on the

Sabbath eve. Otherwise we would have awakened to a cold repast, because no cooking could be done on Sunday beyond boiling the coffee.

When I came upstairs mother was waiting to put a generous portion of oatmeal on the tray that held the rest of father's breakfast. I knew what to do.

Carefully I picked up the tray and carried it to the study door. I knocked quickly but softly, not expecting an answer. I waited a long time, then rapped again.

This time there was a response.

"Come in, son," father said, and I set the tray on a writing table.

Father was clad in the trousers he used when coaling the fire in winter. A sweater was unbuttoned at his throat, and patent-leather slippers were on his bare feet. In his hands was the Bible.

"Thank you, son," he said, and I withdrew without a word.

By the time I had finished breakfast, Eileen was out of the bathroom and almost ready for Sunday school. I began carefully to prepare for church. On Sunday I could wear my knickerbocker suit. Eileen came upstairs from breakfast as I was adjusting my tie. She straightened it for me. Then she primped her big hair ribbon before the mirror and adjusted her long curls.

"Ready?" she asked.

We went downstairs and waited in the living room for mother. She had dressed herself in a gray broadcloth suit and hat, and when she came down and walked smilingly into father's office we knew she wanted him to give her a few words of praise. But this was the Lord's day.

"Everything ready?" father asked.

"Everything."

"God bless you. I'll come home as soon as I can after church so I can change clothes before we go to the Settles' for dinner."

"I know we will hear a good sermon," mother answered. "And remember, dear, if Mrs. Settles isn't in church this morning, don't you dare embarrass her by reminding her she remained home to cook her pastor a Sunday dinner."

She picked up a basket from his table as Eileen and I appeared beside her. Quickly she took inventory of her tools: crayons, pencils, little sheets of green and red paper, two pairs of scissors, three celluloid camels and a donkey, and the *Sunday School Helps*. This was her equipment to teach a Bible lesson to twenty girls aged four.

Without another word we retired, but we did not close the door. We knew father soon would go upstairs to dress, then flee the bedlam of Sunday school by walking in the courthouse yard until time for his service. He did not teach in Sunday school, appearing only on rare occasions when a Rally Day or Mite Box roundup required special exhortation.

Hand in hand, a few steps behind mother, Eileen and I walked from the house, mindful not to slam the screen, and strolled across the yard into the big church. We paused a moment to admire the flowers on the altar, and the sexton hailed us, "The preacher's family are always the earliest."

"We have to get out of the house," Eileen replied bluntly. She and mother proceeded to the basement, where the junior department met, and I slipped out to the street to greet my friends as they arrived.

Promptly at 9:15 the church bell set up a clatter that scattered the pigeons in great circles around the belfry. Doors opened up and down the street, and children, many accompanied by their parents, began to walk to Sunday school. A few carriages came up, the horses at a Sunday trot, but only a few; almost everyone walked, even families who lived on the town's outskirts and on farms near town.

Soon the churchyard was crowded with soap-shining children and beaming adults. This, of course, was only the Sunday-school crowd, composed mainly of youngsters and their teachers. Only half a hundred attended the men's and women's Bible classes. The great bulk of the senior congregation would not arrive for another hour.

A jingle of bells sounded, and I looked up enviously. Roger Haynes, the school superintendent's son, proudly drove up his Shetland at a brisk trot.

Next a humming, noisy for the Sabbath, announced Mr. and Mrs. Jellison, both of whom were Sunday-school teachers. Mr. Jellison always parked his Maxwell directly in front of the church, although he would have denied that, by this ostentation, he was selling cars on Sunday.

Children and adults alike watched the Jellisons alight, then followed them indoors. As always, I lingered behind, delaying as long as possible to avoid the opening exercises that preceded classroom instruction.

From within came strange noises. Through the open auditorium windows sounded the organ, desecrating a gospel hymn. Out of the basement welled the thumping notes of a piano, badly out of tune, and many young voices sang: "Hear the pennies dropping, dropping, count

[82]

them as they fall." From the ugly administrative wing seethed another sound: the strident notes of two pianos, neither in tune, playing separate marches, one for the juniors, the other for the intermediates.

Sunday school had started, in full voice.

Back home, I knew, father was dressing carefully. In a moment he would pick up a leather book containing his sermon notes and walk out into the October sunlight. I did not dare be seen playing hooky from Sunday school, and so I ducked inside the door when I saw him cross the street to the courthouse square, where he would stroll alone for nearly an hour. If I was outdoors, he would see me, for on Sunday morning everyone went to church, including the town loafers who usually sat on the court-house steps. Still reluctant to go to my class, I watched father from the safety of the vestibule. A few of his friends, arriving early for church, passed near him, but they knew better than to disturb. He was immersed in his message, referring occasionally to his notes, and did not even see them.

I went downstairs then, but took a seat just inside the door, in order to be the first one out. At 10:25 the church bell rang again, and I bolted once more to the lawn. Father was still across the street. But now he gazed intently as the children skipped out noisily, each carrying a Sunday-school paper: *Picture Story Paper* for the wee ones, *The Target* or *The Portal* for junior boys and girls, *The Classmate* for the older group. Father was noting how many of the high school students left his church. And I knew he was gratified that only a dozen or so of the vital teen-age children strayed away.

[83]

At the last echo of the bell, he walked back into the house and shut the door. It was his custom to go to his study and kneel before a Morris chair, where, face covered by one hand, he would remain motionless for perhaps half a minute. Then he would rise, carefully rearrange his cutaway coat and wing collar, pluck at his trouser knees, pick up his sermon, Bible, and Psalter, and cross the lawn to the church.

I went into the church then and sat with Eileen and mother. The organ was playing a prelude. Whittier Wilson, the choirmaster, flashed a signal that organist Adelaide Rutherford caught in her mirror. It meant that father had arrived. The organ swelled into the opening bars of the processional, and the choir, in its black robes with white collars, filed into the loft, singing:

> All hail the power of Jesus' name!
> Let angels prostrate fall;
> Bring forth the royal diadem
> And crown Him Lord of all.

With the first words father stepped into his pulpit and knelt for a brief silent prayer. By the time he arose, the choir (which he once described as six voices and a menagerie) was earnestly at work on the third stanza, and the congregation plodded to keep up to tempo.

Throughout the opening hymn father remained seated. He did not join the general singing until the Gloria Patri, which follows the pastor's prayer.

"I like to get my feet on the ground," he explained one time when he was criticized for ignoring the processional hymn. "It is a great responsibility to step into the Lord's pulpit, and I never approach it but my knees tremble a little."

He listened to the earnest singing, and anyone could have read the pride in his expression as he realized that more than six hundred were in church on this particular Sunday. Everyone who should be present on the Lord's day was there, even Abraham Lincoln Nygaard, the paper hanger, whose wife tried to keep him home and often succeeded; and Harvey Whistle, the plumber, who came the first Sunday in each month to pay his church dues.

I watched father surveying the congregation and guessed he was checking up on those who were absent. So many times at Sunday dinner he had described his reactions during the first hymn that I could almost tell what he was thinking.

His eyes rested first on the Amen corner, where the retired ministers sat: three elderly men and one weather-beaten ninety-year-old with a face as stern as the Discipline. Behind them he saw the "mourners' circle" of widowers and, another row back, the Rebecca and Ruth classes of girls in their teens, followed by the teen-age boys, their faces buried in a continued story in *The Classmate*. Father could identify them all, however, by the way their hair was tousled on their heads.

His scrutiny crossed the aisle then to the center section, where, directly in front of him, sat Shiloh Robinson (lightning rods and insurance) with his four-year-old daughter. I could see that he was making a mental note, probably to call that afternoon on Mrs. Robinson and her new baby. Behind the Robinsons were the board of stewards and their wives. Then came two strangers, whom father appraised carefully so that he could give them special greeting after the service. We were next, and I was ready, and returned the wink he always gave me.

Behind us were the entire Haynes family—father and mother, Roger and Louis, Betty Jean and Mary Josephine. Father's face lighted up when he saw them all together, for he liked families to worship together rather than for the children to congregate by Sunday-school classes.

There were other large families, and father checked them all. He lifted his eyebrows when he came to the Millyers. Their second son was absent, and father had mentioned for two days that he must call on Felix in the hospital.

Inevitably father's eyes roamed to the front row left, by common consent reserved for the parish poor family. There, with four of her brood of eight, sat Lily Emerson, without a tooth in her head. The sight of her led father's eye to Foerster Ross, who regularly discharged Lily's husband each Monday for coming to work drunk and regularly hired him back again on Tuesday after a visit from Lily and her whole family. Ralph Emerson was not with his wife. He had taken the pledge three times, but liquor was his strongest obligation.

Father could have looked into the heart and private life of everyone in that auditorium and could have pointed to each one's weakness. And there were so many weaknesses. Instead, it was his way not to see their faults but to commend, whenever occasion afforded, their loyalty in building the church that they now supported so that their children might also worship God the Father and His Son.

In a moment the singing would end. Once more he raised his eyes, but this time he looked over our heads; he was repeating to himself a little prayer he always used at the beginning of his service:

"Father, Thy ways are past understanding. It is a miracle that with only these poor tools Thou hast been able to do anything at all. Thy servants all have been so overabundant with human frailties: Jacob, David, Judas, Peter, yes, even Paul, and now these Thy humble servants gathered together in Thy name. It is a wonder, indeed, that Thy Church has done so much with only human beings to carry out Thy plan. How often must be Thy disappointment. Infinite is Thy patience; God forgive us our weaknesses, and give us strength to do Thy will a little better."

He joined his congregation in the hymn's Amen and arose to conduct his service.

After church father went to the door and greeted his flock one by one. Now and again he jotted down the name of someone who was ill or bereaved or new in the community. He received many congratulations on his return for another year and finally faced Major Cooper.

The Confederate waited until nearly everyone had gone. Then he walked slowly to his pastor and held out his hand.

"Brother Spence," he said, "I'm a sinful old man, and horsewhipping would be good for me except that at my age it'd kill me. You're back, and I aim to cooperate. I decided while you were preaching. If I can't cooperate, I'll keep quiet. You preached a good sermon."

Father shook his head vigorously.

"Brother Cooper," he counseled, "don't you dare keep quiet. The Lord needs a voice to say 'no' as often as he needs one to say 'yes'. I think He's relying on you for the loudest no in this church. Life would be mighty dull, moreover, if I couldn't look forward to a good scrap with you now and then."

They looked each other in the eyes for a long moment, their hands clasped.

"Brother Spence," the Major said, "Lord forgive me, I've misjudged you, even if you are a nigger lover."

"Negro, Major," father corrected, "Negro."

The Major scowled, freed his hand, and straightened his shoulders.

"Negro it is, Parson," he said, and bowed himself out the door.

9

⟨◦⟩

THE first Saturday in November brought a daylong rain, prelude to winter. It began shortly after dawn and by ten o'clock was cascading through nine holes in the parsonage roof.

Father wasn't concerned. All parsonage roofs leak. But rain in the study was new. He was sitting in his Morris chair, working over his sermon notes, when the first drop seeped through from the floor above and fell with an emphatic spat on the shiny oak surface of his desk.

He looked up, surprised. Soon the drop became two, then three. Father leaped up at the fourth and shouted, "Hartzell!"

"Yes, father." The answer was a shout, too, from the basement.

"Did you put a pan of water under that leak in your room?"

"Yes, father."

"Well, go up and empty it. It's overflowing into the study."

I left a bucket of ashes near the cellar door and ran aloft, three steps at a time. The pan in my room lay like a shining island. With speed born of fear over this invasion of father's privacy, I rushed to the bathroom and, seizing the first towel at hand, began to mop up the flood.

But the seepage had gone too far. Father catapulted from his study for a survey of the house. Every time he found another leak he had to go down to the kitchen for a pan. For an hour—scolding, fussing, carrying on imaginary conversations with the parsonage committee—he went from room to room, emptying pans as fast as they filled.

This was no mean task. Two of the leaks were in the attic, well back under the eaves, where even his tall figure scarcely reached. One was in his bedroom, two in the spare room, one in mine, and three in Eileen's, which was exposed to a driving west wind.

Meanwhile mother went serenely about her own work. She had five meals to prepare, including two for Sunday. While she was baking bread, she planned her Sunday-school lesson for the morrow. She had already assigned various Saturday chores to my sister and me. I had to clean the bathroom and basement and finish removing the furnace ashes. Eileen was to scrub the kitchen, dust the house, change the beds, and practice an hour on the piano. All had to be finished by noon, for the Saturday rule of silence went into effect immediately after lunch.

One hour was the usual length of father's patience. He turned the bailing over to me.

"I'm going up and tell Mrs. Sandow what I think of the parsonage committee," he grumbled, wrapping a muffler around his throat. "Let's see if *her* house is dry, and woe betide her if it is."

Out he stomped into the deluge.

The object of his belligerent pastoral visit rarely went to church. "I am too old," she said. Actually she had lost most of her hair and wasn't going to admit it. So little hair remained on her head that even switches wouldn't stay up, and hats would slip down over one eye. She did all her own marketing, heckling tradesmen like an immigrant. She was a familiar sight around town, rattling up the street in a rickety buggy, accompanied by Samson, her coachman. In the heat of driving a bargain her hat would slip off altogether, almost without her notice. But she would not attend divine services.

"I have my morning devotions with my maids and my evening prayers with Samson," she would tell her preacher. "The Lord will forgive me for not going to church."

Lydia Sandow was old, very rich, and had no heirs. She lived in a Victorian mansion atop the town's highest hill, a promontory the Catholics wanted to buy for a new edifice. Her husband had been a successful railroad financier and a congressman and had been handsomely rewarded in both callings.

Only three persons had entree to Lydia Sandow before teatime: her physician, her lawyer, and her pastor. Her church committeework she carried on by telephone, and she was chairman of the parsonage committee.

Unfortunately she could not see leaks in the parsonage roof over the telephone. So up the hill in the rain climbed father, getting angrier every minute, his lips smoldering with words he would use on Mrs. Sandow.

But she was not at home. Her lawyer had driven her into the country to inspect one of her farms, and she would be gone all day.

Determined to find a dry roof, father walked around the drive to the stable and went inside.

The coachman-gardener was sweeping out. When he saw father he stopped in surprise and doffed his cap.

"Mr. Spence!" he exclaimed.

"Hello, Samson," father greeted him, shaking water from his coat. "How nice and dry you are in here!"

"Yes, sir, but Mrs. Sandow, she's not home today. Even in the rain she keeps appointments with her lawyer."

"I didn't come in here to see Sister Sandow," father said, "I came to see you."

Delight and unbelief chased embarrassment across Samson's face.

"To see me!"

"Yes, Samson, just making a pastoral call."

Samson dropped his broom and led the way up a narrow stairway. "But my place is no fit one to receive my preacher."

"Nonsense," father retorted. "A man's home is his inner spirit. All one needs in a house is a roof over his head—yes, a roof over his head."

"My roof," Samson apologized, "will come almost down to your head, Mr. Spence. Mind to stoop coming through the door."

Father ducked low and entered a bright little room with three dormer windows. Picking out a comfortable leather chair, he seated himself and noticed a well-thumbed Bible on a stand at his elbow.

Samson bustled about in a corner and put a kettle on the stove.

"We can have tea in a minute," he said, dropping into a stiff rocker that once had graced the big house. "It's bad out today. I'm honored that you came to see me in the rain. You should have come on a better day. We have just put out a thousand new tulip bulbs."

"On a good day," father observed, "you would be working in the garden or be out and around with your mistress. Today we can talk."

Samson beamed.

"That is so," he admitted. "You are a wise man, Mr. Spence."

When he noticed father glancing around he apologized for his barren quarters.

"You are the first guest I have ever had," he said. "In twenty-two years—no one. We will open the pot of imported Cheddar that Senator Dolliver gave me for driving him to Des Moines. It was a long journey, but we made it without a change of horses. I drove him right up to the new Capitol. Ah, that was a day! Then I came home again and next week from Washington came this package from the senator, with a note in his own handwriting. Let me show it to you."

He went to a drawer, pulled out a letter torn from much handling, and gave it to father. Father took it and read it reverently, as befitted a precious possession. Meanwhile Samson poured boiling water over Souchong tea and ducked into a dusty cupboard for the coveted cheese. When he turned father was looking at him.

"Is something wrong?" Samson asked.

"I can't eat any of your cheese, Samson," father said gently, "and you shouldn't, either."

"Not eat my cheese?" Samson's words were so faint they were barely audible over the beat of rain on the low roof.

"It has wine in it, Samson. The senator's letter says so. You should not partake of anything containing spirits."

"But it is a great delicacy," Samson protested. "In the old country wine is considered food."

"It is a thing of evil," said father. "Wine tempts man to stronger drink, and strong drink leads to sin. We cannot eat it, Samson. Give me the tea, but throw the cheese away."

"Yes, pastor," Samson said. He took the earthen crock, caressed it gently, and dropped it in the ash box.

"The most delicious tea in town," father said.

"Thank you, Mr. Spence. I do not have an opportunity to show it off, you know."

"Samson," father replied briskly, "you are a remarkable man. You haven't missed a Sunday-evening service during my ministry here. I see that you read your Bible."

"It is my consolation."

"You have no friends?"

"Mrs. Sandow, she frowns on them. They cause talk, gossip. She's afraid of gossip."

Father nodded gravely.

"So you live here all alone, never seeing anyone?"

"Mrs. Sandow, she has me in for prayers after supper. On fine days I talk to the maids in the garden. But I need no friends. I have my Bible, my horses, and my flowers. They are enough." He sighed and poured another cup of tea for his guest. "In the winter I fill the conservatory with my friends and visit them there. I have a very old friend, a night-blooming cereus, which is going to reward me by blossoming this January. We are good friends. I call her Matilda."

Father sipped his tea.

[94]

"In the summer," Samson went on, "I have bird friends. Some of my birds have been coming back five, six years. It is welcome to have friends who sing to me."

"Yes, indeed," father interposed, "I have only the choir to sing to me." Then he added prudently, "But don't you ever mention my saying that."

Samson laughed, and father arose to put on his wet coat.

"Would you like to pray before I go?" he asked.

"I would feel greatly honored."

"Never be honored, Samson," Father said, "at the person who offers prayer. All are humble in the sight of God. Be honored at the privilege of praying to Almighty God."

"I am that, whenever I pray."

Father knelt then. Samson did likewise, closing his eyes.

"Almighty God," said father, "we thank Thee for the privilege of walking humbly in Thy sight, for doing Thy Word, for living in the world of Christ Jesus. We thank Thee for the flowers and the birds, for every living and growing thing that enriches our lives and brings us testimony of Thy goodness. Bless Thou Thy servant in this house, and be with him, and comfort him, that his days may be rich and abundant in Thy great love. Take this Thy servant to Thy heart, grant him Thy peace and Thy compassion. Amen."

"Amen," Samson echoed.

They shook hands, and father departed into the rain.

When he returned home, he found a new leak in the kitchen. Each drop that fell sizzled on the coal range.

"You know, mother," he said, seeking and finding her in his study, "we're going to have a new parsonage. These leaks are indecent."

"Yes?" mother queried. "What did Mrs. Sandow say?"

"She wasn't home, but her house was dry," father replied bitterly. "Even the stable was dry. What's necessary for horses ought to be necessary for the preacher. I've had enough of this."

"What are you going to do?"

"I don't know."

"It will be difficult," mother warned him. "The parsonage is so handy to the church you'll never get them to build a new one. Not as long as this one stands, certainly."

"H-m-m," father mused. "That's an idea."

"What is?"

"If this one isn't standing they'll have to build a new one."

"Or rent a worse."

"Impossib e," father snorted. "You know what I'm going to do?"

"What?" Mother's question was automatic. She always let father talk himself out.

"I'm going to get a new church built, right on this spot. Then they'll *have* to build a new parsonage."

"Oh, Will!" mother exclaimed, catching her breath.

"That's what I'll do," father said, steaming with his idea. "We can tear down the church and build a new one so large that it will include this ground. We need a new church. The present monstrosity is sixty years old, and it was a mistake even when new."

"Now, Will, you're not going to build a new church just to get a new parsonage."

"Oh, yes, I am. You watch and see."

He went to the wall telephone.

"And Mrs. Sandow is going to pay for most of it," he added emphatically. "Give me 3182 Green."

He made several calls to men who had talked casually from time to time about building.

"Well, think about it, and pray over it," was the way he left each one. "Pretty soon everyone will be driving an automobile and can come to church oftener. We'd better think about expanding."

When he had finished he looked at mother.

"Well—" he challenged.

"If you build a new church on the site of the old one," she asked thoughtfully, "what will you use while it's building, the courthouse?"

"We could."

"Perhaps Mr. Haynes, the school superintendent, would let you use one of the schools."

"No, he'd charge for it."

Father drummed his fingers on the table in time with the beat of the rain.

"I've got it!" he exclaimed at last. "We'll build a tabernacle. We can erect one for a revival meeting and then use it as a temporary church. It would be a shame to tear it down after the revival without getting other use from it. We'll need a revival, anyway, to get people in the proper spirit to sign church-building pledges."

Next day, however, his enthusiasm died. Before the morning church service Mrs. Sandow drove up to the parsonage and stepped out with her eyes blazing. She swept into the parlor and got down to business.

"Brother Spence," she thundered, "I hear you've been calling on Samson."

"Yes, indeed," father admitted. "A fine and devout man."

"I'll have none of it!"

"Excuse me," her pastor said calmly. "I didn't hear you correctly."

"Oh, yes, you did," Mrs. Sandow whipped him. "I said I'll have none of it."

"You mean," father exploded, his eyes beginning to take fire from hers, "that I cannot call on Samson?"

"You may not," she said, sweeping her long purple skirt around her toes. "Why, I'll be the laughingstock of the whole town. Do you realize just what you've done?"

"Yes, indeed."

"You've put Samson on my social plane," she raged. "You are my pastor, and you will call on me. My coachman belongs in the stable."

"But your coachman is also a member of my church."

"Not at all. He attends the evening service."

Father gripped the arms of his chair.

"Sister Lydia—" he began.

"Don't you 'sister' me," she snapped, flicking her head in his direction so that her hat toppled about her eyes. She smashed it back onto her head again.

"Tell me," father said, trying a new tack, "don't you have Samson in for evening prayer?"

"I do," she answered. "I also have prayer with my maids. As mistress of the house I am responsible for my servants, and that includes their devotions. But I don't invite my servants to tea! And I don't expect them to invite my friends to tea with them."

[98]

"But we are all children of God. There is no distinction in His sight. 'As ye would do unto me, do even so unto the least of these.' "

Mrs. Sandow rose, stiff-backed and haughty.

"Don't you start quoting Scripture at me," she blazed. "You ministers are all alike. You find a precedent in the Bible for everything, even sin. If Samson wants to go to church to save his soul, that's one thing. It's different entirely for my pastor to call on and have tea with him."

[99]

"I'm sorry, Sister Lydia," father insisted, "but I cannot agree with you."

"Then," Mrs. Sandow announced, gathering her skirts for a plunge through the door, "you are no longer my pastor. From this day on I'm a Baptist."

She slammed the front door after her.

10

By NIGHTFALL Sunday the news was all over town. Lydia Sandow actually had been seen attending the Baptist service.

The Baptists buzzed with excitement even more than the Methodists. They were more stunned than if Michael O'Connor, the saloonkeeper, had asked for immersion. Baptist elders desecrated the Sabbath quiet by calling on each other to seek the implications. Baptist laymen idled past the parsonage, hoping to see father and question him.

As for father's congregation, one by one the women dropped in or telephoned to impart the awful news.

As usual, in cases of intense excitement, father put his children to work. Eileen was assigned to answer the front door, and I was stationed at the telephone. As soon as a parishioner walked up the front steps Eileen summoned mother, who went to the door and smilingly took the message. My task was to keep those who telephoned from reaching father, unless they were unusually important or insistent. When they were, father resorted to his usual strategy—to make the caller laugh.

"She'll never consent to an immersion unless they take her to the River Jordan," he would say. "She was baptized a Methodist, she married a Methodist, she'll die a Methodist. She'll be back."

But the furore continued unabated.

After an hour of nearly continuous calls the telephone girl said briskly, "Your father's as busy as I am. Here's another one."

I called father again, and he went wearily to answer. "Sometimes I wish this plagued thing had never been invented," he said. Then he suddenly relaxed, for the caller was Dr. Romer, who wished to know if father needed help. Dr. Romer always quieted father. They were kindred spirits. Father still thought he himself might have been a great surgeon, and Dr. Romer had put himself through medical school by preaching in country churches. Their interests naturally drew them together, and they had become a team. The doctor kept father's medical knowledge up to date and let him help diagnose cases, and father loaned the doctor his newest theological books.

"Doc," he said, "what I need is a telephone girl."

"The rumpus is as bad as that, is it?"

"It is. I haven't had time to think about my evening sermon."

"When are you going to start? It'll be a tremendous job."

"Holy smoke," father exclaimed, "are we talking about two different things?"

"I don't think so. All I've heard about all afternoon is the new church."

"The new church!" father gasped. "What about the new church?"

"Some of the men met with me after service. We went at it hot and heavy. But we've decided to do it. I'm calling to let you know—"

"Oh!" father groaned.

"Come, come, what's the idea? Why, I backed the plan to the hilt. Don't you want a new church?"

"Of course I do, but I never imagined the idea would catch on so fast. Where will we get the money? Have you thought of that?"

"Well," Dr. Romer chuckled, "we have a good idea for *some* of it."

Again father groaned. Mrs. Sandow's generosity endowed almost every phase of church life. Without her money the plan for a new church was in peril. "Then you haven't heard about Mrs. Sandow?"

"My land, she's not dead?"

"No, nothing like that. She's gone over to the Baptists—I thought everyone knew by now."

"Well," Dr. Romer said dubiously, "maybe we'd just better sit on the new church idea awhile."

"Maybe we had," father echoed and hung up thoughtfully.

"Well," he sighed to mother, "if there's anything else to disturb my evening sermon I'd like to know about it now."

Mother smiled. All day she had been meaning to tell him, but discretion had persuaded her to put it off. Now the time had come.

"Then you might as well know," she said, "that I'm going to have a baby."

On Monday it became apparent that the Baptists

didn't want Mrs. Sandow. Even Hoseah Carmichael, the Baptist pastor, was against her.

"We will not turn away anyone who wants to worship with us," he confided to Major Cooper when they met in front of the courthouse, "but she has come to us with a vengeful heart, and we cannot baptize her."

The major hurried to the parsonage and told father. He also imparted the news that Mrs. Sandow's withdrawal had aroused the Methodists as had nothing in twenty years. The whole church was indignant. They would show Mrs. Sandow that they could build a new edifice without her help!

When father fully realized that he really had a church building program on his hands he hunted for mother to tell her. She was hanging the washing on the clothesline.

"Mother," he called, anxious because she was doing such heavy work in her condition, "how do you feel?"

"Oh, very well, indeed," she said.

"You'd better conserve your strength. We'll get Lily Campbell to come in and do the washing and ironing."

Mother, her mouth full of clothespins, pointed to a wet sheet in her basket. Quickly father picked it up and blunderingly swung it over the line.

"Here," he said, "let me do the rest. You just tell me how."

Mother pointed, and he set about her work, talking the while.

"I've a brilliant idea," he said.

"Sh-h-h" mother cautioned, "remember the O'Connors next door."

"Why don't we teach old Mother Sandow," father continued in a boisterous whisper, "a lesson she'll remember the rest of her days?"

porary house of worship to serve while the old building was torn down and the new one erected. The budget for the new church was set at $100,000, an astronomical sum in that community. Finally the quota was leveled off at $60,000. It included a bell tower but no bells and a choir loft but no organ. Already father was assigning a few items to Lydia Sandow. But Mrs. Sandow remained aloof, though hinting through a few friends that if her pastor would apologize she would return to the fold. Father pretended not to hear.

Only one serious argument arose over the plans. The Discipline forbade any levity within the sanctuary; Mr. Haynes, Dr. Romer, and many parishioners with growing boys, on the other hand, insisted on a parish house with a gymnasium. They proposed that it be built on the ground occupied by the present parsonage.

A genuine Methodist fight developed. Father quoted the Discipline as an argument against any such nonsense as a recreational center. Church members pointed out that the gymnasium could be used for socials and Sunday-school classes as well as for amusement. Moreover, organized recreation within the church would keep Methodist youngsters out of pool halls and be an incentive to Sunday-school attendance. There could be a rule that only those children who attended regularly could use the gymnasium.

Through meeting after meeting father stood his ground, Discipline in hand. When finally Dr. Romer realized that no persuasion would budge father, he slipped over to the parsonage to consult mother. He left humming a bright tune.

That night, when the debate was at its fiercest, he arose.

"Brother Spence," he began with a convincing air of resignation, "you are the pastor of this church, and so it is you who should make the final decision. We have argued long enough. I have changed my mind and am willing to bow to your judgment. Besides, if we don't build a parish house, we won't have to tear down the parsonage and, therefore, will not have to build a new one. Remodeling the old one will save a great deal of money. You are right, Brother Spence."

Father recoiled and looked at Dr. Romer as though seeing Judas. With his right hand he fumbled for the Masonic emblem on his watch chain, a clear signal that he was badly hit. Then, slowly, he rallied and cleared his throat. If going without a gymnasium meant forfeiting the new parsonage, obedience to the Discipline must go.

He sought now and found a way to save everyone's face.

"Perhaps this is a case," he reasoned, "in which we should lead our church into a broader interpretation of human values. My only argument against a parish house with a gymnasium is the Disciplinary admonition against levity within the church. But what you have said about the need for clean fun for our children is true. I guess we should pioneer. Let us prove that this tenet of our Discipline should be revised. We'll build the gymnasium."

The day in early spring that the tabernacle was dedicated climaxed one of the busiest periods in father's life. Rising unusually early, he went out, without shaving or eating, for a last look at the tabernacle. Mother ran after him.

"Will," she called from the porch, "I've just got to see you today. It's very important."

Father turned. "What about?" he asked.

"I can't shout it into the street," mother answered indignantly. "Do you realize we have scarcely seen you for weeks? You have a home to run as well as a church, and your home has problems, too. I *must* see you this morning."

Father frowned. From his pocket he took his appointment book and a pencil.

"Let me see," he considered. "All right. I'll be home at ten o'clock for half an hour." He wrote mother's name in the book.

Mr. Jellison, driving to his salesroom, picked father up in his Maxwell.

"Everything set today, Mr. Spence?" he asked.

"Yes, everything's set. The district superintendent will be in on the eleven o'clock train to make the dedication address."

"It's a good idea," Mr. Jellison said, "having the dedication at noon. The children will be out of school, and the merchants will be able to attend."

"It is important," father affirmed, "that the children attend the dedication. After all, we are building the new church for them more than for ourselves."

They pulled up in front of the tabernacle, on a vacant lot in the church block. A long, low structure, sixty feet wide and half a block deep, it had been built without foundation excavating. The supports rested on the ground, and the cheap pine on the sides and the sharply pitched roof were covered with black tar paper.

Well," father beamed, "there she is!"

"Yes," echoed Jellison, "there she is, and we'll be in her for a year, I guess."

"The most momentous year of our lives, Harold," father went on, "and the busiest."

Jellison patted the steering wheel of his car.

"Mother and I talked about our pledge last night," he said. "I think we can stretch it to $500. These cars are beginning to sell now."

Father knew that $500 to Harold Jellison, whose two sons wanted to study medicine, would mean the long-time sacrifice of everything but the meager necessities of life.

"God bless you," he said, much moved. He stepped from the car and admired it. "This thing certainly whisks you around in a hurry. Now that I live so far from the church, I ought to have one."

Jellison's eyes gleamed.

"You certainly should, pastor."

"I could make twice as many calls in a single day as I do now if I had a car and still have time for the building program. It would really be worth it to the church."

With a sigh father waved Jellison on his way and stepped into the tabernacle. The finishing touches were being put on the altar. Father walked briskly up the unfloored aisle and tested the altar rail with his 185 pounds.

"Better make that a little stronger," he told the carpenters. "We're going to have a revival meeting in a few weeks, and if I know this town that rail will be heavy with sinners."

Next he went over to the courthouse to see Mr. McAfee, the clerk of the court.

"I hope," he began, "that you can get away today for the dedication."

"Oh, yes," Mr. McAfee smiled, "the whole family will be there."

"Good. I just dropped by to remind you."

"Well, that's mighty nice of you pastor, with you so busy and all. I appreciate it."

Father started for the door, then remembered something.

"Oh, by the way," he said, "I'm not getting many weddings now that I live so far away. Are you sure you're telling people how to get to my house?"

"Yes, I tell them, but Mr. Schroeder, the German Lutheran preacher, lives on the way, and he has a sign on the porch with his name on it. From the look of the returned licenses, most of your weddings are going over there. You'd better get a sign of your own."

"I will," said father. "Meanwhile I don't suppose you could route those couples up Third Avenue, could you? They could turn at Maple Street, on the *other* side of Mr. Schroeder's house."

"Why, of course," said Mr. McAfee, and father went to his church office well pleased.

Three men were waiting. He disposed of their needs quickly and efficiently and then greeted Dr. Romer, who had dropped in on his way to the hospital.

"I'd give my right eye to see that operation this morning, Jack," father told him, "but I can't make it. The dedication is taking all my time."

"All right," Dr. Romer said, picking up his bag, "but I think I'll have something for you to see next week—a patient with a gastric ulcer that hasn't responded to medical treatment. I'm going to operate—a gastro-enterotomy. There are complications, and I think you'll find the case very interesting."

[111]

"Count on me," father said. But as Dr. Romer put his hand on the door to leave, father detained him. "Say, Jack," he said hesitatingly, "I wish you'd go over my heart one of these days soon. It's skipping a beat at times."

"So?" Dr. Romer asked with concern. "You'd better ease up, boy, you're working too hard."

"I know, and with this church building program on I'm apt to be going at top speed for a long time. I can't spin around in a car the way you do. I have to walk."

Dr. Romer nodded seriously. "We'll have to do something about that."

Punctual about appointments, father arrived home on the stroke of ten. He went directly to his study. Mother followed.

"It's about Hartzell," she explained. "His school-teacher is sending him home. He has been fist-fighting with his schoolmates, and she hasn't been able to stop him. He's such a little boy that he has to show the bigger boys he is as strong as they. Miss Edmonds wants you to talk to him. Don't be too hard on him, she said, but point out that he must obey the school rules."

"I don't see," father protested, "why the schools don't permit fighting during recess. It's manly and teaches many lessons. These new-fangled school notions are all nonsense."

"But, Will, as long as there are rules the preacher's son must obey them."

"That's right. When he comes in send him upstairs. I'll be shaving."

When I entered father was busy with a straight-edged razor. He pointed toward the bathtub, and I sat on its edge.

"How's school going?" he asked casually.

"All right, sir."

"Are you being excused from class today to attend the dedication?"

"All the Methodist kids get an extra hour off at noon."

"Children, not kids," father corrected.

"Yes, sir."

"What are you studying now?"

"Sums and reading, mostly. I hate arithmetic, and I hate drawing."

"What do you like, then?"

"I like reading very much."

"Anything else?"

"I would like writing, but they won't let me use my left hand."

"We'll see about that," father promised, surveying his freshly shaved face.

"I like stories about places I've never seen. Some day I'm going to see them all. I'm—"

"Son," father interrupted, beginning to whet his blade on the razor strop, as he always did after shaving, "what have you been doing on the school ground to cause Miss Edmonds to send you home?"

"Fighting."

Father continued stropping.

"Were you told not to fight?"

"Yes, sir."

"And you continued?"

"I couldn't help—"

"Son," broke in father sternly, "don't tell me an untruth. Whatever you do, stick to the truth. You kept on fighting, didn't you?"

"Well—"

Father set down his razor but kept his hand on the strop.

"This strop," he said, "has more than one use. It will sharpen a razor. It also will sharpen a boy's ability to do as he's told."

He unbuckled the leather from its hook, seized me by the arm, and administered capital punishment. But there was no sting in it.

"I can hit much harder than that," father warned me. He was trying not to smile. "Now, go back to school."

I I

꧁ ꧂

THE revival meeting has undergone many changes since its early days. There was a time when the followers of John Wesley were known as "the shouting Methodists" because of their vocal response to religious exhortation.

Even when I was a boy certain preachers had standard phrases they relied on to provoke cries of "Amen," and any evangelist who didn't "raise the roof" was not invited back another year. The old-time revivalists loved spontaneous encouragement. Today a minister would feel heckled if his congregation interpolated loud shouts of agreement during his discourse.

I remember an elderly Methodist bishop who worked for an hour and a half to thaw out a prewar congregation. He tried all his tricks but met only stony silence. Exasperated, finally, he interrupted his sermon to ask, "Are those bald heads I see down there or tombstones?"

No one answered.

"You, brother," he said, pointing to a man in an aisle seat, "have you a voice?"

The man nodded but did not speak.

"Then use it, man, use it," the bishop begged. "How

[115]

does the Lord know you are a Christian unless you shout out the glory?"

His listener merely looked uncomfortable.

"Praise the Lord!" shouted the bishop. Even that drew no reaction. Again he pointed down the aisle.

"Can you say 'Praise the Lord'?"

"Why, of course."

"Then *say* it man, *say* it."

The man said it.

"You *whisper!*" the bishop roared. "Is that all you think of the Lord? Can't you *shout?* Come, now, follow me. *Praise the Lord!*"

This time there was a faint echo.

"That's better. Shout it now, *louder.*"

The man shouted.

"Hallelujah!" cried the bishop. "Everyone in the auditorium, now, repeat after me, and use your lungs! Hallelujah!"

The reaction was half-hearted but promising.

"That's the spirit. Again, with all your might. Hallelujah!"

"Hallelujah!" came the answer.

"Now, after me: Praise the Lord!"

"Praise the Lord!"

"Now once more: Amen!"

"*Amen!*" This time the answer was tumultuous.

The bishop mopped his brow and smiled. "That's better," he said. "I was afraid for a moment I was addressing heathen."

There is a story told of a circuit evangelist in the early days of Indiana Methodism who spent two solid hours exhorting his backwoods audience to repent. At the altar call only a few timid women came forward. Angered at this lack of faith, the preacher glared about the church, then shouted, "I have a deep impression that some young man or woman in this house will be tramping the streets of Hell before I come again." The penitents' rail filled quickly.

Father was as much responsible as anyone in Methodism for a change in revival technique. He never exhorted anyone to be good lest he roast in Hell. Rather, he made the avenue of Christ so tempting that his congregation wanted to walk it with him.

In his regular sermons father usually chose a New Testament text: one in which the Christian way of life was a thrilling experience. During a revival father continued along this tack, though in his early ministry he usually brought in a professional evangelist to exhort those parishioners who responded only to the threat of brimstone, as had their fathers, when Hell fire was needed to compete against the worldly excitement of free land and Indian murder.

Father's revival-meeting strategy always was the same on the first night. He worked on his regular church congregation. Graphically he recalled all the sins, both of commission and omission, of which his flock was guilty.

So profound was his understanding of human frailties, needs, and longings that every sermon he preached was personal. He never referred to an actual case, of course. But many in the congregation thought he did, and, as he was preaching, people would look furtively about to discover how many persons besides the pastor had discovered their secret sin. Sometimes half a dozen members would take personally the same remark and hasten to repent.

"I could tell whom I was hitting by the way they looked over their shoulders to see if the family skeletons were sitting behind them," father said years later. "And sometimes members would become angry and stay away, believing my sermon was aimed directly at them."

At the first revival meeting in the new tabernacle, father emphasized the need for an annual renewal, just as the housekeeper puts her home in order and the businessman takes inventory. Then he hit his parish amidships.

"How many of *you*," he asked, leaning across his pulpit intimately, "have been uncharitable toward a neighbor or have not settled a quarrel? How many of you have neglected your children's religious training because you were too lazy to get up in time for Sunday school? Do you harbor a grudge against a business competitor? Have you overworked your employees or your hired girl? Can you come to the altar of Christ with a pure heart? Or is your soul so crowded with little sins that there is no room for Christ?"

He let that message sink in while the choir, always augmented for revivals, chanted softly:

> Just as I am
> Without one plea,
> But that Thy blood
> Was shed for me
> And that Thou bidd'st me
> Come to Thee,
> O Lamb of God, I come, I come!

Father held up his hand. The singing stopped, but the organ continued the hymn. To its accompaniment father spoke: "There probably is no one here tonight who is not trying to live as Jesus would have us all live. But we are human, and we have sinned. Forgive us, O Lord."

From the retired-ministers' corner came a loud "Amen."

Responding to this reaction, father lifted his voice slightly. "There is probably no one here tonight who deep in his heart doesn't want to let Christ in. Open our hearts, O God."

Again came the "Amen" from several directions.

Father stepped from his pulpit to the altar rail.

"I ask all those who earnestly want to follow Christ to join me here at the altar. Let God and your neighbors know that you humbly repent your sins and that you earnestly desire to live the Christian life. Come!"

The choir sang the hymn again.

> Just as I am, and waiting not
> To rid my soul of one dark blot,
> To Thee, whose blood can cleanse each spot,
> O Lamb of God, I come, I come!

Nobody moved. But father knew the courage such a declaration required. He was in no hurry.

"We are assembled here," he resumed, "in a new tabernacle. Before us lies a year that will test our faith. Give us courage, O God."

"Amen!"

"We will need greater faith, greater love than ever before. Give us that faith, O God."

"Amen. Amen."

The congregation was a little restless now under the enchantment of the minister's voice and the repetition of the hymn.

Father walked up and down before the altar, then spoke again.

"I remember a man who once said to me: 'Brother Spence, why should I be saved? I am already saved.' My answer was: 'Brother, conversion redeems a man from the sins he *has* committed. But many a man thinks that because he is saved he can do no wrong and, thus encouraged, he develops new sins.' I have no doubt that many of you here tonight believe that because once you were saved you will forever remain in grace. That is not true. Salvation must be renewed. You need to cleanse your hearts anew. Your pastor needs to cleanse his own heart. Who will join me as I confess my own weakness?"

Father knelt at the penitents' rail, and again the choir sang. Three retired preachers came forward and knelt beside their pastor. Emboldened, a few church members slipped from their pews. Soon a score or more were kneeling.

The visiting evangelist then stopped directing the choir and stepped to the pulpit. That year he was Wilson Keeler, a famous exhorter who brought his wife as organist and his son as tenor and trombonist.

" 'Come unto Me,' " he said softly, " 'all ye who are weary and heavy laden, and I will give you rest.' How often you have heard those words. Yet how many of you actually come to Christ? How many of you are so proud of your Heavenly Father that you will publicly declare your desire to renew your Christian faith? Will *you* come?"

They came. The organ played. Father arose and went in turn to each penitent to whisper a few words. Mr. Keeler continued his persuasion.

[120]

"There may be many here tonight who have always tried to live the Christian life but have never publicly declared their Christianity. How often have we heard the words: 'I am not ready yet. Wait a little while.' When I was in Michigan last year a beautiful young mother attended many of our meetings, but she would not come forward. 'I am not ready yet,' she said. This year I returned to her town and asked for her. She was dead. And I was deeply touched. Once too often she had said, 'I am not ready yet.' Now it is too late. We never know when our turn may come. I may be next. You may be next. God grant that we may be ready. Come! Do it now, while the Hand is upon you! Do it now, that your heart may be at peace. Don't let the Devil struggle with your soul. Wrest him out and come to Jesus. Come and see how serene your life will be with God in your heart. Don't put it off. Don't say you are not ready. Come!"

They came.

The choir sang other hymns: "Rock of Ages," "Amazing Grace, how sweet the sound that saved a wretch like me," "My faith looks up to Thee, Thou Lamb of Calvary," and "O Jesus, I have promised, to serve Thee to the end."

Father and Mr. Keeler alternated at the exhortation, with little anecdotes out of their own experience, simple emotional pleas that touched every kind of sinner. In half an hour, when all the church stalwarts had renewed their faith, father dismissed the congregation with a stirring prayer in which he begged God to lay his hand during the revival on all who needed salvation. Then he kept the penitents a little longer for another prayer, and the three retired preachers saw that all filled out a card detailing their names, addresses, and church affiliation, if any.

Rarely was the first night anything but a renewal of faith for regular church members, although a few stray sheep were rounded up. Father would use those saved on the opening night as an inspirational group that sifted through the audience in the course of the following meetings. During altar calls thenceforth little scenes occurred all over the tabernacle.

Mrs. Welch, who had been fighting with her neighbor over a boundary dispute, but could not sue her because the Discipline forbade Methodists from suing each other, slipped into the pew beside her adversary one night and put an arm around her. The two wept quietly for a minute; then Mrs. Welch led her neighbor to the rail and knelt with her.

Mr. Cambridge, angry for weeks at a parishioner who had bought a piano from a competitor, went to his enemy and shook his hand. The two talked for a moment, then went to the rail.

One night Mrs. Baker saw, sitting alone, a young woman who had applied at her millinery store for a job. Mrs. Baker went to her.

"You are Mrs. Salverson, aren't you?"

She nodded.

"May I help you?" Mrs. Baker whispered. "Perhaps if you tell me what's troubling you, it might help."

Wrought to an intense emotionalism by the repeated altar calls and music, Mrs. Salverson cried bitterly. "I can't do it any longer," she sobbed. "Night after night I have come here, but it does no good. I think of my two little children hungry at home. If God was as kind as

[122]

these men say, wouldn't He keep my babies from starving?"

Mrs. Baker tried to put an arm around her, but Mrs. Salverson drew away.

"I have tried desperately to get a job," she said. "But nobody needs me."

"Have you no husband?" Mrs. Baker asked.

Mrs. Salverson shook her head. "He died a year ago and left nothing."

Tears filled Mrs. Baker's eyes.

"God bless you," she said, "I am a widow, too, and I have very little, but you are welcome to share it. I will find work for you."

A moment later Mrs. Baker led Mrs. Salverson to the altar.

One night, when the hammering of rain on the tabernacle's wooden roof echoed across many empty seats, Major Cooper spied a vaguely familiar face in the congregation. He finally placed it as that of Reuben Wright, once a regular churchgoer but now never seen. The major hobbled up the aisle and slid into Wright's pew.

"I haven't seen you in some time."

"I haven't been here," Reuben Wright scowled.

"Have you been out of town?"

"No."

"Have you been sick?"

"Let me alone," Wright said.

The major sat silently beside him for a long time. The altar call continued. The music swelled. Mr. Keeler's son played softly on his trombone an old hymn: "Jesus is

[123]

tenderly calling, today. Calling oh, sinner, come home."

Wright stirred. "I haven't heard that for a long time," he said.

The major nodded.

"I was just thinking that, too."

"Do you remember," Wright asked, "how Wesley Carmichael used to play it on the cornet in Sunday school?"

"So he did," the major recalled. "Why, that's fifteen years ago!"

"Yes," Wright replied, "it's been a long time."

"But it would be good to hear him again," the major said. "I wonder if we could get him to play it Sunday? If we could, would you come?"

Wright hesitated. "The church has outgrown me. It doesn't want me around any more."

The major remembered now. Wright had stopped attending church when the choir had been reorganized eight years before. Wright's voice was gone, they had said. A flicker of sympathy came into the major's eyes.

"They don't need me, either," he said, humbly. "I no longer do anything except attend the Sunday service. And I get mighty lonely, sitting there by myself. Why don't you come out next Sunday and join me? It would help. Maybe we could organize an old duffers' Bible class, and you could teach. You used to discuss the Scriptures wonderfully, I remember."

Reuben Wright looked at the major for the first time. "Do you think we could?"

"Why not?" the major asked. "There must be others, like us, who have grown away."

"There's the Widow Jordan," Wright said. "She

[124]

hasn't been to church since Albert died. There's Harry Gray—you remember him—"

"And Lizzie Carson," the major added, "whatever happened to Lizzie Carson?"

"We ought to find out," Wright suggested.

"Let's do it."

It was Wright now who sought the major's hand.

"You know," he said, "I've been hoping for years that I could get back to my church. I've missed it."

A moment later they walked up the aisle together. Father knew from their faces that something extraordinary had happened and gave them a special blessing.

Another rainy night brought an entirely different scene. Foerster Ross, entering by a side door, hung his wet coat on the end post that supported the altar. The corner was dark, since gas lamps in the tabernacle were centered as much as possible. After the sermon father, as usual, filled the rail with penitents and at the end of the service sent them to their seats. As usual, too, before his benediction he glanced up and down the rail, for sometimes a sinner, wrestling with a particularly heavy sin, remained at prayer after everyone else had gone. This night, in the dim corner by the door, he saw a figure hunched into a coat, head bowed so low it was out of sight.

Quietly father addressed the meeting. "We still have one soul at the altar. If upon his conscience there is a grievous burden, he needs our help. Let us all pray silently that he may recover his faith."

The organ played softly one verse of a hymn.

"Amen," father said, but the penitent did not rise.

Father waited a moment, then prayed aloud for mercy on the sinner. Still there was no response. Again father waited, then gave a broader hint. "Go in peace," he said, "and may the Lord go with thee."

Still nothing happened.

Thinking perhaps the man had fainted, father walked over to the dim corner. He put his hand on what should have been a shoulder and touched a post.

Unabashed, he turned to his flock, which by then realized what had happened.

"Let us not be dismayed," he said quietly, "that we have lifted up our prayers for an empty coat. Now you know how I feel, night after night, praying for living, breathing souls in this tabernacle who could respond and will not."

12

THE second week of the revival found father's composure completely gone. Night after night he was in the pulpit. Day after day he made pastoral calls upon the redeemed. By Saturday noon he was in such a state that we dreaded to sit at the table with him.

After lunch we children went out to play quietly in the yard, and mother retired to her room. Suddenly a shiny Maxwell touring car stopped in front of the house. Father joined us in a flash, fatigue and inability to concentrate over a sermon utterly forgotten. He was half way down the front walk before Harold Jellison had set the brake.

"A little tribute to our minister from a grateful congregation," was Jellison's greeting.

Father climbed behind the wheel to see if there was room for his long legs.

"This is the finest thing a church has ever done for me," he beamed, giving the wheel a possessive pat. "I deeply appreciate it."

"The car's not yours, you understand," Jellison warned. "It belongs to the church, but it's for your exclusive use."

"Of course, of course," father replied. "Come teach me how to operate the blooming thing."

But that remark was just for the family. He had been practicing over back roads for nearly a week. Off he drove with Mr. Jellison.

After the service next morning father relaxed. The revival had ended and there would be no evening devotions. The day was beautiful with the warmth of spring.

Immediately after dinner Eileen and I begged for a ride in the new car. Father looked at mother.

"What do you think?" he asked.

Noting the sparkle in his eyes, she gave the correct answer: "The Discipline says nothing against driving a car on Sunday."

"I think, however," father said soberly, "we should weigh the question very carefully. The automobile is something new in our lives. It is not a thing of evil, but it could be put to evil purpose. If we go for a ride on Sunday afternoon, church members may say, 'The pastor uses his car on Sunday,' and find in that an excuse to drive in the country during church hours."

Mother had anticipated that difficulty. "The automobile also can be used to bring people to church who live too far away to walk."

"That's true," father agreed. "But if people drive cars on Sunday, soon they will be buying gasoline on Sunday and fixing tires and profaning the Sabbath with ungodly amusements. We must not encourage that."

"No, but we can fill the gasoline tank for the Sabbath on Saturday, just as we buy groceries on Saturday. Now that the automobile is coming into general use, we should be an example for the church to follow."

"True," father admitted.

"It would be better for the children to be out riding quietly on Sunday than playing noisy games."

"True," father repeated, still hesitating. Usually when he deliberated the answer turned out to be "no." His affirmative judgments invariably were quick and sure. Our hearts sank.

"I think we should go," mother said quietly. "It is the only way I can get out now. And I may not be able to go out after today for some time."

"Great Scott," father exclaimed in dismay. "Why, mother, I—why, I've been so busy with everything I almost forgot—" Mother's warning glance stopped him. "Forgive me," he concluded tenderly. "Of course, we'll go for a little ride. Are you sure it will not be too much for you?"

"I shall enjoy it."

Father arose, and we rushed for our coats.

"But remember," he cautioned us, stern again, "this ride must not in any way disturb our usual rule of a quiet Christian Sabbath."

Six miles out in the country the car gave a snort, jumped, and stopped.

"What the mischief?" Father got out, took the crank, and spun it until he was out of breath. Then he sighed, "I don't know what's gone wrong."

"Do you suppose," mother asked, "that we have used up all our gasoline?"

"Probably. I don't know how long these things go before you have to fill them up."

By now we were all out of the car. Father looked anxiously at mother and asked, "Are you all right?"

"I'm fine," she smiled. "The Brookses live only a half mile up the road. Let's go there."

When we arrived the astonished Mrs. Brooks looked at mother and gasped, "Land sakes! Come into the kitchen and have some tea. No wonder we didn't see you at the revival, Mrs. Spence."

Mr. Brooks offered to hitch up a team and take us back to town, but father refused. The horses were entitled to their day of rest, too.

"If you can put us up and Mrs. Brooks won't be put to any work, we'll stay the night," he said.

"Of course, we can put you up," the farmer replied.

It was noon next day before we returned to the parsonage. Mother went to bed immediately, and father stayed close to his study, but not too close to see me when I returned from school in the afternoon.

"What are you eating, son?" he called out.

"Candy," I answered, holding up a chocolate cigar.

"Let me see it." He took the cigar as though it were an evil thing. "Where did you get this?"

"Down at the corner. Mr. Jansen sells them for a penny, but he gave me this because I didn't have any money."

Father regarded the chocolate thoughtfully.

"I don't think, son," he said finally, "that you ought to have this kind of candy. Chocolate is all right. A little after school is good for you. But I don't like you to be touching anything that looks like tobacco. It might tempt you later to buy a real cigar, and smoking is sinful. I'll just throw this away."

Tossing the cigar in a wastebasket, he put his hand in his pocket and brought up a penny.

"Here," he said, "get something else."

Mother came down to a dinner cooked by Lily Campbell, the temporary hired girl.

"What was the final report on the revival?" she asked, heading off the question father was formulating about her health.

"Fine, fine," he boomed, cutting the roast. "Six hundred and seventy-five cards were signed. A hundred and three were strangers with no church affiliation. We have eleven new members."

"Isn't eleven a very small number out of so many converts?"

"Yes," answered father ruefully, "I guess we held the revival for the Presbyterians. Most of the converts are going over there."

"Why?"

"The Methodists, mother, are building a new church. You can't expect a sinner to mend his ways and sign a building pledge in the same year."

After dinner mother went upstairs with us to tuck us in bed. But tonight she did not take down the *Life of John and Charles Wesley* or any of the big brown-backed books from which came wonderful stories of Beowulf and Mowgli. She kissed us both and sat down in a rocking chair by the window.

"When you wake up tomorrow," she said simply, "you probably will have a little brother or sister, and I will be in the guest room. Be as quiet as mice, because we will be very tired. There will be a nurse named Miss Gratz. You do everything she tells you, and be good children."

She walked out and closed the door.

Eileen called across the room, "Do you know where babies come from?"

"From Heaven," I answered promptly. Father had told me they came from Heaven, and father was always right.

"Pooh, that's not it."

"Where, then?"

"You're too young to know," my eight-year old sister said, and I could get no further words from her.

In the morning father stopped pacing the floor to greet me at the foot of the stairs.

"Son," he said, "you have a baby brother. Your mother is sick, so don't make any noise." His hat was on his head, his watch in his hand; he was ready to prance downtown to spread the news, but something held him back.

"Aren't you going out?" I asked.

"Well, son," he fussed, "there's one trouble with being a preacher. When other men have new sons they can go around passing out cigars, but I—"

His eyes lit up suddenly with an inspiration, and he patted my shoulder. Without another word he rushed from the house, went down to Jansen's on the corner, bought a pocketful of chocolate cigars, and strutted up and down Main Street, bursting with his good news.

"Here," he greeted each friend, "have a cigar."

As the friend registered shock, then amusement, father grinned with delight.

"That's just like you, Brother Spence, to think up a good one," everyone said, proud of a pastor who was not above a little joke.

Father ate up the applause and was in such a fine mood when he came home for lunch that he put his hands on my shoulders affectionately and invited me, too, to have a cigar.

"When a son is born," he explained, "it is fitting to do something very special. Your grandfather would have invited everyone in for a dr— for a drop of tea. But we can't afford that. Some men give out cigars to their friends. We can't do that either. So just this once—in honor of your baby brother—I have given away *our* kind of cigar. I want you to have one, too."

He pressed me to take the chocolate, but I was too confused to yield.

"That's fine, son," father said finally, nodding ap-

[133]

provingly, "stick to a principle. But in this case you don't really need to. It's all right."

Still dubious, I no longer refused the cigar. But I didn't understand at all.

My brother's baptism was so long delayed that it almost became a public scandal.

Three months passed. An unseasonal heat as of midsummer was on us, and mother was teaching Sunday school again before brother received his christening.

Mother wanted him named for father. But father was still sensitive that he had been named just plain William Spence. A middle initial that stood for nothing would not do for his new son. He insisted the child be called William Fraser Spence, after an illustrious uncle. "Not," he reminded mother, "the one that was hanged for horse stealing."

Meanwhile brother was called Baby, and the wonder of members grew until one day Eileen's schoolteacher went so far as to question her.

"What will be your new brother's name?" she asked in front of the class.

"Oh, we don't know," Eileen replied glibly, "but one of his names will be Spence."

This comment caused so much laughter when the children carried home the story that father decided to force the issue with mother. He announced from the pulpit that new babies in the church would be baptized the following Sunday. Still mother would not budge. Brother was brought to church, nonetheless.

Father had a formula for baptismal services. He *had* to run off all of his service, including the baptism, with the precision of a modern radio program in order to end on the stroke of noon from the courthouse clock. He called the parents and children to the altar and started at the left of the line. As he approached each mother he leaned down and asked in a whisper, "What is the baby's name?" Upon receiving the answer, he baptized.

When he came to mother she was more firm than ever, for every other child was accompanied by both parents, and she stood alone. Father smiled proudly at his son and leaned over to ask the usual question.

"William H," she answered, tightening her protective hold on the baby.

Father nodded, straightened up, and took water from the grail.

"William Fraser Spence," he said, "I baptize thee in the name of the Father, the Son, and the Holy Spirit."

Mother was furious, but could do nothing. She returned to her pew, indignant. Straight ahead she stared, defying father to look at her. He became unusually busy with his notes and began his sermon. But he would finally have to look at her, and she knew it. For all during his ministry her telepathic encouragement was his mainstay in the pulpit.

He looked. Mother's eyes were so stony that he stammered and glanced quickly away. Around the tabernacle, up one aisle, down the other, he glanced until at last he must return to mother. Still she glared. He began to stumble, sought his notes, but had forgotten to turn the pages, and so was lost. Helplessly he appealed to mother again. And in the face of his desperate need she relented. The fire in her eyes went out. Her face relaxed. She looked at him with an expression that said clearly, "I forgive you."

Father, too, relaxed. The confidence returned to his voice, and, without again referring to his notes, he finished his sermon.

After church the family went home ahead of father. He seemed unusually delayed. Finally he appeared.

"Thank you, mother," he said, as she helped him off with his Prince Albert coat, "it was more than I deserved."

13

༄

THE three months during which Fraser went un-
named were busy for father. Once the tabernacle was in
use, wreckers began razing the high, slate-roofed building
that had housed the parish for fifty years.

The town newspaper was full of the details. When the
steeple came down there was a picture on the first page.
When ground was broken for the new building the paper
donated $100.

"The work of Christ," an editorial said, "deserves the
support of the whole community. The edifice which is
being erected on the corner of First Avenue and Maple
Street will, like this newspaper, enrich our community
and guide its thought long after those who read and write
these words are gone."

Bishop Quayle, a spellbinding orator of the circuit-
rider school, delivered the sermon when the cornerstone
was laid. The congregation stood on the street for two
hours while the bishop preached to the greater glory of
Methodism. The newspaper carried his sermon in full. A
$5,000 gift from United States Senator Dolliver, himself
a church member, inspired another story.

By the end of September the outer structure was taking shape. But the congregation was in serious trouble. Hard times had settled down over the community. Hogs brought scarcely enough to pay the cost of shipping to Chicago. The farmers tightened their belts against a hard winter, and the merchants sat in deserted shops.

Promises of money for the new building, made in emotional enthusiasm nearly a year before, became difficult to keep. Many pledges were cut; others were defaulted entirely. Those who did pay deprived themselves, and to meet the growing deficit a few of the more fortunate went into their pockets again and again. Father dipped into his own, too, far more deeply than he had any right to do.

Father reported at Conference in October that completion of the new church would be delayed indefinitely. None of the other ministers envied him his charge now. After Conference he returned to Fort Dodge to find the men in a fever over a contract for the new church plumbing and the women semihysterical about utensils for the kitchen in the gymnasium.

Foerster Ross, who should have been low bidder for the plumbing, was nearly $2,000 higher than Downey Brothers and Tweed. This would never do, for Mr. Tweed was an Episcopal vestryman, and the Downeys actually took their children to see motion pictures. Father rejected all the plumbing bids on the excuse that they were excessive and reminded Ross of his obligations as a church member before calling for new bids. Ross responded by trimming nearly $3,000 from his previous estimate, and father, with a sigh of relief, turned his attention to the Ladies' Aid.

[138]

The ladies, who were responsible for equipping the kitchen, were not to be so easily handled. Mrs. Cambridge, the president, was an incessant talker and insisted on telephoning father about each petty complication. In order to forestall interruption, she would talk without pause for five minutes and then hang up with a bang. Even with a new desk telephone that eliminated the necessity of getting up each time the bell rang, father was annoyed. He soon learned to say merely, "Yes, Mrs. Cambridge," when she greeted him, then put down the receiver and resume his work. When a click issued from the telephone he put the receiver back on its hook. This went on for three months, during which time he did not interfere. But when it became apparent that the women would never get together father wrote to the general church architects and from them received the specifications for a model kitchen, which the Ladies' Aid accepted.

Meanwhile, Mrs. Sandow felt completely out of the excitement. Everywhere she went she heard about the new church: how Mrs. Weeks's new fall coat had gone into the building; how Mrs. Harvester and Mrs. Lang were fighting over whether seat cushions would be proper in the pews. But Mrs. Sandow did not dare to express her opinion. Ideas and opinions were the private property of paying members.

All winter and spring, while the town was clamped in a shell of depression, the new church stood vacant, its outer structure complete, but unfurnished within. Worship had to be continued in the frigid, barnlike tabernacle. Father preached sermons of hope, and Sunday after Sunday the congregation responded, singing with fierce fire:

[139]

Blessed assurance, Jesus is mine;
O what a foretaste of Glory Divine.

Father would return enthusiastically from each service and exclaim, "We never had such singing. It takes sacrifice to make God's word live. These people really are living their Christianity. I can feel the strength of it clear up in the pulpit."

Then suddenly Europe went to war. The prices of corn and hogs bounded, and the Methodists took new hope. Each European battle headline boomed farm prosperity. Money flowed again, for as the farm goes so goes the Iowa town. The farmers knew that if the war lasted until fall prices would continue to rise to a new "high."

Within a few weeks pledges were being paid, and the building was on its way to completion, including the furnishings.

The church dedication was a great day. Great because of the work that had preceded it, the battles fought, the sacrifices made. The bishop himself and the district superintendent were on hand to share this glory of Methodism. Father was in the background, but it was he who contributed the master stroke.

The service began in the old tabernacle, now weather-beaten from two years of use. The place was jammed. An overflow of several hundred stood outside.

Father, his cutaway coat particularly pressed and a white carnation in his buttonhole, opened the service alone. The choir was ready but did not sing a processional. Father stepped into the bare pulpit without a trace of excitement. He opened his Psalter and read the call to worship:

"'The Lord is in His Holy Temple: let all the earth keep silence before Him.'"

Then, before anybody could sit down, he lifted his arms for quiet and read a simple prayer of confession:

"Almighty God, unto whom all hearts are open, all desires known, cleanse the thoughts of our hearts with the inspiration of Thy Holy Spirit, that we may perfectly love Thee, and worthily magnify Thy Holy Name, through Jesus Christ our Lord."

The choir chanted an Amen.

"Almighty God, from whom every good prayer cometh, deliver us from coldness of heart and wanderings of mind; that with steadfast thoughts and kindled affections we may worship Thee in spirit and in truth, through Jesus Christ our Lord."

Again the choir sang Amen.

With a gesture wide enough to include all the hundreds present, father announced calmly: "Will the choir follow me." Then his voice, without instrumental accompaniment, boomed out in the most stirring processional hymn he knew:

> Lead on, O King Eternal,
> The day of march has come.

Fifteen hundred throats—inside the church and out—caught up the hymn, and carried it on:

> Henceforth in fields of conquest,
> Thy tents shall be our home;
> Through days of preparation
> Thy Grace has made us strong,
> And now, O King Eternal,
> We lift our battle song.

Eyes proud, figure erect, his whole being alive with glory in the accomplishment of Christ's work, father walked slowly up the crowded aisle and down the street. To the steps of the new church he marched, the choir and congregation behind him.

In five minutes an auditorium built to hold twelve hundred was packed. Father then gave a signal to open the folding doors into the gymnasium, where there were three hundred more chairs. Before the offertory they, too, were filled.

The visiting dignitaries now took over the service, and father had an opportunity to look around. Here was a church to preach in: a giant hall built in a semicircle, with a balcony all the way around; overhead a great dome with blue stained windows, through which a May sun filtered. On his left was the huge organ loft, in which an old piano looked woefully out of place. But it would do until an organ could be purchased and installed. Behind the piano was a large window of plain glass. It, too, would suffice until it could be replaced by a tree-of-Jesse window.

Attentively father followed the district superintendent through the Order of Service and listened as the bishop began his sermon. The bishop was coming to our house for dinner, and father would have to discuss the sermon with him. But within two minutes he knew he had heard the sermon at General Conference three years before.

So he transferred his interest to the congregation. First he sought out members to see how they were reacting. Then he looked for strangers. In each pew he had placed a card that read: "If you do not belong to any church, and wish to become a member of this one, sign your name and address, place it in the collection plate, and the pastor will call." He wondered how many would sign.

Then he discovered Mrs. Sandow. She was 'way at the back on a gymnasium chair. Father looked twice to be sure of what he saw next. Samson was sitting beside her.

Father smiled. Many months previously he had actually ordered a carillon that would cost $25,000, confident that, in the end, Mrs. Sandow would pay for it. But he had had no guarantee that she would, and he knew that he had acted on a very rash impulse. The circumstances inspiring him to do so had been such, however, that he had not regretted his recklessness, though he had had many anxious hours about the outcome.

Some time after Fraser's baptism Mrs. Sandow had sent word to father, through Samson, that she would like to see him. When he arrived she greeted him with the amazing confession that she had been "a sinful old woman."

"Have you been neglecting your prayers?" asked father.

"Oh my, no. I mean—because of going to the Baptist church."

"I don't see any sin in that," father parried. "I think Brother Carmichael's flock will get to Heaven as fast as we will, and he is a good preacher."

"But not like you, Brother Spence."

"People don't join a preacher, Mrs. Sandow. They join a church. They take the preacher the Lord sends them and give thanks for the privilege of worship, even with the kind of preachers the Methodists have."

The thrust hurt, and Mrs. Sandow immediately changed the subject.

[143]

"Brother Spence," she said sadly, "I'm very unhappy. I feel that each day I'm slipping a little farther away from God."

"You probably are," father commented drily. He knew that a nature such as hers responded only to roughness, and so to help her he was compelled to be blunt.

"Have you no sympathy?"

"You don't need sympathy. Self-pity is a work of the Devil. You need a little old-fashioned religion."

"That's just what I mean! The old-time religion!" Her face brightened, and she sang in a cracked voice, her head bobbing from side to side:

> The old-time religion
> The old-time religion
> The old-time religion
> Is good enough for me.

How nearly that had got him! He had braced himself and looked out of the window in order not to notice that her switches were falling completely away from her bald spot. When she put them back in place, he said, "I'm afraid I can't help you. Your trouble is of the inner spirit. Until you have humbled yourself before Christ Jesus and come down off your high horse, nobody can do anything for you."

"What *can* I do?"

"That's up to you."

"Don't you *want* me back?"

"Frankly," father said, utilizing the opportunity to set her thinking, "the church is at peace for the first time in years. We are all working now, not just a few, and we are *all* sacrificing. Christ's work is carried on by sacrifice, Mrs. Sandow."

"God has forgotten me," she whimpered.

"No, Lydia," he corrected her. "*You* have forgotten *God*. You must cleanse your heart and learn humility."

Father rose and boldly flung open the great walnut sliding door that gave onto the room where Thaddeus Maximus Sandow had died. The room was sacred to Sandow's memory, and was opened only on the anniversary of his death.

"Your husband was a sinful man, Sister Lydia," he said. "But when the pride burned out of him he found greater richness in the love of Christ. His last ten years were an example to this community. In our new church we should have a mighty carillon to peal out across the town as his goodness rang out, to rich and poor alike. But that is impossible. Go in to your husband, and learn from him."

He had left, then, without another word, but he had been so sure of her reaction that the next day, in a burst of enthusiasm, he had ordered the carillon. In all the excitement of completing the church building he had almost forgotten the incident.

But as the bishop concluded his sermon father realized with a jolt that the bells would be delivered in less than a month. The time had come to settle with Mrs. Sandow.

14

FATHER decided to wait until after noon the next day before calling on Mrs. Sandow; he did not want her to suspect his purpose by appearing too eager. So on Monday he bustled off to his new office in the church building, after outlining to mother at breakfast his plans for a strenuous morning. But she was not impressed. She knew he could not work in a study ten blocks removed from her, with no one to talk to except the janitor.

Father admired his new quarters, but the empty stillness soon got him. Instead of the work he had planned, he began sorting the cards he had placed in the pews the day before and organizing his new members by streets and districts so that he could call on them without waste motion.

By noon this task was completed, and he returned home for lunch with the name of Lydia Sandow at the top of his calling list. Twice during the meal parishioners telephoned to tell him a new joke about the big belfry without a bell and the choir loft without an organ. But he alone knew these jibes were a two-edged sword, and he set out for the Sandow mansion in an unusually serious mood.

As he drove through the pretentious entrance gates he saw Mrs. Sandow tying a vine on the portico. He stopped before her, and greeted her jauntily, "Good afternoon, Sister Lydia. It's a beautiful day."

"Indeed it is," Mrs. Sandow called, "do come up on the porch and sit down."

But father did not allow himself to be trapped into observing the amenities of a social call.

"Thanks," he replied, "but I can't stay. I came to see Samson."

"He's in the garden. I'll call him."

"No, no, don't bother, please. I'd rather talk to him out there."

Mrs. Sandow was disappointed, and also curious. "What do you want to see him about? Maybe I can help you."

"It's church business," father replied firmly.

That hurt. "Come in just a minute," she entreated. "Then you can see Samson."

"No," said father, "but I'll drop in on the way back."

He went around to the back of the house and found Samson spraying rose vines. "No one can grow roses as you do, Samson."

The gardener dropped his sprayer in surprise, then doffed his hat in homage.

"I've come to see you at your work," father said. "It gives me strength to see a man helping God's flowers to grow. One can get nearer to God out of doors."

"Yes, I've found it so," Samson agreed. "If you like these flowers, I could bring some Sunday. Mrs. Sandow, she lets me do anything I like now."

Father smiled. "That brings up my real reason for calling on you."

"Yes?"

"I want you to be chairman of a new committee on altar flowers. We should have flowers every Sunday, and you know what would be appropriate and how to arrange them."

"Oh, that would be a fine thing," Samson was infinitely pleased, "but let Mrs. Sandow be chairman, and let me do the work."

He cut a rose and placed it in father's lapel.

"Samson," father said, "you are one of the most loyal members of my church. You give to it beyond your means, and you work for it. You are the chairman."

"But Mrs. Sandow, she'd be better——"

"I have other plans for her."

"In that case," Samson yielded with a quick bow, "I am honored. You have never seen such flowers as I will grow for you. Ah, it will be fine to send my beauties to the altar of my church!"

Having accomplished this mission, father returned to the big house. He noted that Mrs. Sandow had changed her dress and added generously to her hair.

"Well," father asked, "how do you like the new church? I saw you at the service yesterday."

"It's big and beautiful, but may I say it's cold?"

"Ah," father responded, "you would be the one to notice that. 'Most everyone else just admires it because it's new."

"Brother Spence," she beamed, leading the way to the parlor, "I don't want to interfere, but the church really needs an organ badly. Now don't mistake me. Miss

Rutherford is doing a splendid job with the piano. But it just doesn't seem right, somehow, to hear a piano in that church."

"That's perfectly true, but we are lucky to have the church. If this war hadn't come along, we wouldn't be in it yet. We'll just have to sneak up on the organ—and the chimes."

"Yes," she agreed, "I've been thinking about what you said. Remember?"

"What I said?" he echoed vaguely.

"Yes, about a memorial to Thaddeus that would ring out all over town. Sometimes I lie in bed almost believing I can hear those chimes, and I catch myself thinking, if he were alive he would so proudly give you the chimes, and the organ, too."

Father reached for his hat.

"Oh, Brother Spence," Mrs. Sandow pleaded, "let me give the chimes and the organ."

"No, we can't do that. We must all work together toward that goal, the way we built the church."

"But—"

"No, I'm sorry, Sister Lydia. The church would never allow it."

"Why?"

"Well—" father hesitated, "it would cost a lot of money. The Skinner organ we want costs $10,000, and the carillon, when it arrives from Switzerland, will call for a payment of $25,000. That's too much for one member to bear."

"Oh, no, I could do it. I'm old now. I can get along with less."

"No," father declined, "it wouldn't be a good idea.

People who have scrimped and saved to give $100 would feel very badly if you gave so much. It would make their gifts seem very small indeed."

"Then let me do it anonymously."

"They'd guess."

"You could say you raised the money from new sources."

"That would be untruthful. No, Sister Lydia, it just can't be done by any member of the church. If you want to leave it in your will, that's a different thing."

Here Mrs. Sandow balked. "Then I'd never hear the bells."

Father rose. "Well," he said, "I must be going. It's very generous of you to make the offer, and I will let our people know. But they'll never accept, if for no other reason than that it might mean giving up all those jobs you used to hold. I think they'd rather not."

Mrs. Sandow drew herself up. "I will never be like that again, Pastor. Night and day I have prayed in my husband's room, as you suggested. I shudder sometimes to think what the church put up with from me in the old days."

"We will be glad to have you back," father said invitingly. The time to be gracious had come. "There is no reason why you cannot renew your church subscription."

"I was going to attend to that today," Mrs. Sandow said hastily. "I'm going to double it."

"That would be very generous. We are desperately in need of funds to keep the new church going. And—" father paused and looked at Mrs. Sandow intently, "if you would like to give a tree-of-Jesse window in your husband's memory I'm sure no one would be hurt by that gesture—in memory of Thaddeus."

"Brother Spence," she cried excitedly, "I will." Then another inspiration came to her. "And Thaddeus will give the chimes and the organ. In his will he left a memorandum that if a new church ever was built, *he* wanted to contribute—"

Father closed his eyes as he did in the pulpit just before each sermon. "That was very generous and far-seeing of your husband," he said quietly. "On behalf of the church, I accept his bequest."

Father was the first person in town to play the chimes. Not only did he have such an accurate ear for pitch that any discord hurt him physically but he could play almost any instrument that was put in his hands. He was accomplished at the piano, organ, and violin. Many times I have heard him working off his temperament on the piano. He used to wander into Mr. Cambridge's music store and play whatever came to hand. Once Mr. Cambridge tried a prank. He had just received a new instrument, a xylophone. Leading father to it, he said: "Here's one you can't play." Father took the mallets, looked at the blocks, tapped one of them to get his pitch, then confidently struck off, without a flaw, the tune of "Lead, Kindly Light." On the second verse he played chords.

The carillon was no problem at all. He watched the mechanic put the keyboard together. Up and down the ladder father followed him from the control room to the bell tower, supervising the installation of each bell. At last the job was done. Father turned to the craftsman.

[151]

"Is it ready, now?" he asked, his hands already on the levers.

Without waiting for the answer, he began to play "The Church's one foundation Is Jesus Christ our Lord." He could not have chosen a more difficult tune, for it used every bell in the tower. But he played without a fault. People came to their doors up and down the street. The crowd left the veranda of the hotel a block away and stood on the sidewalk. Few of his listeners had ever before heard a chime.

When he had finished the mechanic exclaimed, "Where did you learn to play one of these things? I've installed two dozen and never heard a better player."

Father beamed. Dust was across his face, cobwebs on his suit. His hands were dirty. Without answering, he played again "In the Cross of Christ I glory, Towering o'er the wrecks of time. . . . " At the end of the tune he stopped. Up from the street came voices, picking up the second stanza:

> When the woes of life o'ertake me,
> Hopes deceive, and fears annoy;
> Never shall the cross forsake me:
> Lo! it glows with peace and joy.

Father listened the verse through, his head high. Then he went to the window and looked down. The street was filling with people.

He turned away, tears in his eyes.

"If the chimes can lift those drummers off the hotel porch and get them to singing hymns in the street," he said, "God's work has indeed been done."

Installation of the organ fascinated him, too. A newspaper reporter, seeking information about the new instrument, found father flat on his back in the bellows room, holding strips of felt for Mr. Beaston, the technician in charge. Mr. Beaston not only was the best organ repairman in Iowa but, like father, was high in the Consistory, one of the branches of freemasonry. Father watched every detail as the organ was set in place and again was the first to play it. So delighted was he with its tone that he could not wait until its dedication, when Clarence Eddy would come from New York to show it off in a recital. He got the jump on everybody, but in a humble way.

It was father's habit to make Communion services available to his parish occasionally on Friday afternoons as well as on Sundays. One of these services was due now. The church organist usually could not leave her work to play the Communion music. So father had learned how to administer the sacrament and supply the music, too.

On Friday he let the church fill with the devout until more than one hundred were present. Then he stole up to the organ loft and began to play softly. For nearly half an hour he played, using the *vox humana* so liberally that the auditorium seemed filled with human voices. When he was sure that all traces of daily toil had been erased from the supplicants' minds, he slipped down to the altar and administered the Communion.

Never in his entire ministry was the sacrament received more devoutly. Members remained long at the altar and returned to their seats instead of hurrying home. When all had partaken, father went again to the organ and played quietly until the last person had departed.

At the formal dedication of carillon and organ, when the bishop again was on hand, father realized, with an overwhelming sense of desuetude, that his job was done.

Mrs. Sandow sat humbly in a front pew. She cried a little as the bishop praised her late husband's many benefactions and again when Clarence Eddy let the organ out in a Bach toccata that vibrated the crystal chandelier in the church dome. Father strengthened her with an encouraging smile.

But everything was too peaceful. There was no challenge ahead: nothing to plan for, to fight for, to worry over. For the first time in his ministry, he sat behind the pulpit and was bored.

The bishop noticed father's attitude and was pleased, for he wanted father to tackle a new job. After the service he took father into the study and told him that in a neighboring state was a parish that was surrendering to worldliness, a condition he believed father might cure.

"I'm not asking," the bishop said as father's imagination leaped at this challenge, "that you go to Omaha. I just want you to think about it. There will be no decision anyway until Conference time, and that's almost six months away."

"I'll think about it," father said fervently.

15

AFTER his talk with the bishop about the Omaha church, father refused for days to discuss anything else. He even lost interest in the new parsonage, which was almost complete, a fine home in an attractive residential section, four blocks from the church.

Mother had no desire to move. She wanted to enjoy the new parsonage awhile and give the lives of her children a little permanence. Artfully she tried her usual tricks, which heretofore had never failed.

"You're not looking at all well," she would say to father. "You've nearly worked yourself to death. Now that you have a perfect church organization, a new home, and a car, you'd better take things a little easier for awhile."

But anything less than top speed was unknown to him.

"I'm not going to stagnate," he replied. "Look at Dr. Karlquist. He's been at Kelsie for ten years, and he's covered with moss."

A few days later mother pointed out that the new hospital Dr. Romer was building, just two blocks from the church study, would offer a wonderful opportunity for father to enjoy his interest in medicine.

"You are just throwing temptation in my way," was his retort.

All one afternoon mother read the papers and *The Literary Digest* carefully, and when father sat down to dinner she presented a strong argument against his becoming uprooted during a war.

Father listened patiently, proud of the way she built her case. But his conclusion was blunt: "When a minister takes root he is through."

"Have you ever considered the children?" mother rushed on. "They scarcely know what it is to have a father. Sometimes I think I have neither a husband nor a pastor. I'm not a wife, certainly, just a housekeeper taking care of a widower's children. It's not fair to tear your wife from her friends and put your children in strange schools every few years."

"That's Methodism," father answered with finality, but he was badly shaken. An hour later a dozen roses were delivered to mother. The accompanying card said: "From your man."

Omaha, however, continued to be a challenge of destiny, a "Call" that he felt he was preordained to answer.

When mother realized his thinking had gone that far, she surrendered.

"All right," she prophesied, "but you will be unhappy."

Father's reply was to gild the only feature that made mother look with any favor at all upon the change. This was the increased salary that it would bring.

When father and mother had first moved to Iowa father was paid four times a year—if he could collect it. Just before the quarterly visit of the district superintendent (who came primarily to get his own share) the church stewards put on a strenuous campaign to raise the "quarterage." Some members pretended that "quarterage" meant twenty-five cents and dutifully paid out a "quarter" four times a year. Others who had no cash paid their pledges in vegetables or poultry, upon which they set their own price. They would bring the produce, unsolicited, to the parsonage. So we often ate chicken we could not afford but had no money to buy medicine in times of illness. Once father carried a ten-cent piece for five weeks, not daring to spend it, for it constituted the family's entire cash reserve.

The result was that we were forced to live on credit most of the year. Since the Discipline forbade preachers from falling into debt, father patronized only his parishioners, pointing out that he was taking from them provisions only up to the total of their annual church pledges.

When father's "settlement day" arrived he received his three-months' salary from the church treasurer in a sack, into which nickels and dimes, many quarters, and a few one- and two-dollar bills had been stuffed as they were collected. Father knew the treasurer never bothered to count these collections: the total was never sufficient.

Usually father was paid at the end of the day after the bank had closed. Father and mother would pull down every blind in the house and count the coins to find out what percentage of the salary actually had come to hand. Then they passed a sleepless night, for if they were robbed they would be hopelessly in debt, without a penny to tide them over the ensuing three months. They would put the sack on the parlor table and sit up all night watching it. If father dozed mother would let him sleep

[157]

for ten or fifteen minutes until her own eyes became heavy, whereupon she wakened him and took a brief nap. Every creak in the house was a terror, yet mother would not let father investigate, because then she would be left alone with the moneybag.

One summer father hid his quarterage overnight in the stove, and one winter he concealed it in a bleak corner of the attic. But at Fort Dodge he faced no such necessity. For eight years he had been paid, as he expressed it, "in full and on the nose." Twice a month his salary check was in the mail. And father believed that this method would be continued at Omaha, except that the checks would be substantially larger.

Even after we moved into the new parsonage at Fort Dodge father continued to talk of Omaha, and long before Conference he had decided to make the change.

When the time came to announce father's departure the Fort Dodge congregation was stunned. As Mrs. Cambridge said, "We can't imagine the church without Mr. Spence. We think of it more as *his* church than our own."

The usual farewell reception followed and was held, of course, in the church gymnasium. Families to whom father had ministered far beyond the demands of his profession wept unashamed as they said good-by.

"If we weren't all packed up," father told mother with tears in his eyes (the emotional strain was almost too much for him), "we wouldn't go."

But we went. And Omaha was all that mother had predicted. The church was suburban, perpetually under the shadow of "First Church" downtown, and father did not like to be in shadow. That, however, could have been endured if the suburbanites had been like the people of the prairies. They were not. They were city dwellers in every sense of the word: worldly, rarely emotional, without enthusiasm for anything except a new game called "bridge." Father knew how to minister to the openhearted farmers and townspeople of the plains, but this urban civilization defeated him. He did not take kindly to Sunday golf, speculations in stocks and grains, and war profiteering.

Seeking desperately for some way in which to make his mission a success, he decided upon a revival meeting that would blast his congregation loose from its attitudes, but the official board rejected the idea.

"We don't want any display of emotionalism in our church," they said.

Finally one day, after a fruitless round of pastoral calls, during which he found no one at home, father gave up the fight.

"Mother," he said, "this isn't a church at all. But with the help of Almighty God and the undertaker, I'll make it one."

From that day he settled down to a strategy of watchful waiting.

He had fumed against the indifference of his congregation, but far more upsetting was the begrudging manner in which his salary was paid. It was held back often despite the fact that many church members lingered in the vestibule after service to boast about how wealthy the war was making them. But delay was not the only distress. When father did receive his pay, or part of it, he had to undergo humiliation.

The church treasurer was the president of a large

insurance company, Malcolm Rickey. His wife owned a race horse. Rickey never once mailed father's check. Each time he, his wife and his daughter, rolled up to the ugly parsonage in their Hudson Super Six and made a call that lasted all evening. Then, as they were leaving, Rickey patronizingly pulled father's stipend from his pocket.

"Your check, Mr. Spence."

This so infuriated father that after each such visit he had to walk around and around the block for an hour before he was calm enough to retire.

As the weeks went by and father's church activities diminished he began to relax, much against his will. He was richly rewarded. To his astonishment he discovered that he had a family. We children were delighted, for we in turn learned what it was to have a father.

The closer we got to father the more we began to coax from him favors that in his busy days he would not have allowed. We persuaded him that playing outdoors on Sunday was not evil. Then one Sunday afternoon Eileen made a pan of fudge. With trembling hands she took a few squares on a plate to father in his study.

He looked up, saw the tempting chocolate, and reached for a piece. "Did you make this all by yourself?" he asked. "It's very good."

Emboldened by this new intimacy with father, Eileen and I began coaxing for a great favor. Our playmates attended the Saturday-morning movie at a neighborhood theater. We had never seen this wonder. For half the winter we begged and were rebuffed with quotations from the Discipline on worldly amusement.

But finally the children's favorite, Marguerite Clark,

was billed in *The Seven Swans*, a story mother had read to us at bedtime.

"I don't see how that could hurt the children," mother said.

Father went to the library, took down the book of fairy tales and read the story through. Then he telephoned the theater manager.

"Is this picture you are showing to the children clean?" he asked. Assured that it was, he continued, "Does it follow the fairy tale exactly?"

It did.

Father walked up and down for a long time, Eileen and I watching. Finally he turned to us and said, "All right, just this once."

When we arrived at the theater, which was packed with children, the program had been changed. The fairy tale had been delayed in transit, and in its stead was a Theda Bara picture, the chief episode of which, so far as father later was concerned, involved the seduction of a bank teller.

Father was on the porch when we returned.

"Well?" he asked. Glowingly we explained the wonders of the motion picture and the plot of the story. But when we reached the seduction, father broke into a rage.

"I thought you went to see a fairy tale," he boomed. He spent the next five minutes behind closed doors talking by telephone to the theater manager.

After that movies were forbidden. But, having experienced their fascination, I could not stay away. I began to sell *The Saturday Evening Post* from house to house in order to secure money to attend a nickelodeon specializing in Western pictures.

Of course, father soon heard about it.

"Son," he said, calling me into his study, "I hear you have been going to the Bijou Theatre."

"Yes, sir." Our new familiarity did not allow falsehood.

"Well," he sighed, "the fault is mine. I allowed you to go to the first one. So it is up to me to show you I was at fault. I am going to *take* you next Saturday and point out, in the film itself, why it is not good for you."

When Saturday arrived father accompanied me into

[162]

the theater as resolutely as though he were entering a saloon in response to a call to attend a dying drunkard.

It was a William S. Hart picture. Cattle rustlers roamed the lawless Oklahoma plains, pillaging and sinning. They stole cattle and ranchers' daughters. They crowded the saloon and caroused. At each such episode father nudged me.

"There!" he grunted. "Is that an example you want to follow? Can you lend your presence to such an exhibition?"

I said nothing, of course.

Finally the outlaws whooped into town on a Sunday morning while the preacher was blazing away with wholesome Methodist vitriol. Into the church the outlaws rode, pulled the preacher from his pulpit, sat him on a horse and headed him out of town. Father sat tensely and forgot to nudge. Bill Hart rescued the minister and used the outrage as a springboard for organizing the law-abiding citizenry into a posse to restore law and order. Edna May Oliver, as a rancher's wife, stormed the saloon and dragged her husband out to join the vigilantes. At this scene of a righteous woman fighting for the right to worship, father chuckled, then silently watched the two-gun hero ride the outlaws down. At last the villains were safely locked in the town jail. Hart claimed the minister's daughter as his bride, and father laughed with delight.

All the way home I waited for his reaction. At the front door it came. "There *is* a good moral there," he said.

I heard no more until the following Saturday. Shortly after lunch he invited me to go to the theater with him again.

To mother's uplifted eyebrow he responded, "It will do me good to relax before my Sunday sermon."

16

❧☙

ALL winter father continued to be happy with his family, surrendering his dignity so far as to slide with Eileen on her sled down Woolworth Avenue's long hill; but only after dark, of course. Then an issue arose, and he abandoned play for work.

The Anti-Saloon League had become active in our suburb. For several weeks father joined the prohibitionists in addressing meetings, praying before doors of saloons, and soliciting money. But when the campaign crept to the door of his own church he balked. His policy was to support all agencies that strove for the betterment of mankind or the relief of suffering. For this reason he helped the Y.M.C.A. in its drive for funds and eagerly assisted the Community Chest, the Salvation Army, and the Children's Milk Fund. But he always insisted that he had done his part when he opened his parishioners' homes to such appeals. Under no circumstance would he open his pulpit to them.

When Maurice Billings, the state Anti-Saloon League's secretary, said that he would like to preach in father's church the following Sunday, father nodded amiably.

"You can preach, certainly," he said. But when Billings added that he intended, after the sermon, to take up a collection, father denied the request.

"May I ask why?"

"A pulpit," father explained forthrightly, "is the fountainhead of public worship from which a sermon on temperance may be preached. But it is neither a soapbox nor a collection plate."

Mr. Billings had never heard anything like that before.

"Then you aren't with us," he concluded, emphatically.

"I *am* with you," father assured him," heart and soul. I will give freely of my time and energy. But no one has ever taken a collection from my pulpit, and no one ever will."

Billings was speechless.

"Suppose you preach your sermon," father suggested, "and in the afternoon go out into the parish and ask for financial support. I'll help gladly—but let's keep the solicitation out of the pulpit."

Mr. Billings arose, angrily.

"From the way you talk," he snapped, "I'd almost think you wouldn't even appeal for Red Cross funds or preach a sermon on the war."

"Indeed I wouldn't!" father retorted. "The church is for the worship of God and for the message of Christianity. For *no* other purpose."

"Then you must be pro-German!"

"Let's not evade the real issue," father answered.

"I think the *real* issue has just been uncovered," Billings said meaningfully and asked to be excused.

[165]

The next day the entire community knew that father was a pro-German.

Such an accusation, in the spring of 1916, could lead only to disastrous consequences. The papers daily reported incidents illustrating, all too clearly, how the populace had become inflamed. At Grinnell College a professor's house was painted yellow because he dared ask a class in psychology to be neutral. In another town a Y.M.C.A. secretary was excoriated because he suggested that, instead of going to France with a relief unit, "Y" secretaries should stay at home and prevent America from sending her sons to war. Even a strictly neutral stand was dangerous.

Father, being a Canadian by birth, had cousins, college classmates, and boyhood friends "somewhere in France." Many had been killed in action. But he had resolved that no martial words would emanate from his pulpit.

On the day the awful stigma was first hurled at father he was on the porch, watching a squirrel crack acorns. A neighbor passed, and father called a greeting.

The neighbor's response was to shout the dreaded epithet "pro-German!"

Father went white and gripped the porch rail with both hands until his accuser had passed. Then he walked into the house haltingly, went to his room, and closed the door.

When he emerged, mother went to him anxiously, but he was calm again.

"I've been called the Devil's disciple and a lot of names I won't repeat," he said with an ironical smile. "I guess one more won't do me any harm."

But he made no attempt to joke about the matter with his parishioners. Taking his silence for guilt, they relayed the accusation. Those who did not believe its truth, nevertheless helped to build the case against him merely by repeating what they heard.

Father's friends advised him to preach a ringing sermon in support of the Allied cause and, incidentally, his own.

"The pulpit is the font of God," he replied. "I will not use it for any except God's purpose, and especially will I not use it for self-defense."

He continued his usual sermons of salvation and redemption and the blessed mercy of Christ Jesus. In the face of his inspired Christianity the resentment dwindled but did not cease altogether.

Ultimately, he bought a new Ford touring car and drove off on a secret mission. Back he went to his Iowa Conference. When he returned he was happier than he had been in some time.

"Mother," he said, smiling broadly, "I think we'll be invited to a new church soon."

Several weeks later he received a telegram from an Iowa friend: "Would you consider Morningside College church in Sioux City? College youth perturbed by war need inspirational guidance."

The call of youth excited mother as well as father. Her heart was in the religious education of the younger generation, and at Morningside, a Methodist college town, her opportunities would be limitless.

"What shall we do?" father asked.

"Let's go!" she exclaimed.

"Amen," father answered and rushed to the telegraph office.

Then passed an agonizing week during which father became pessimistic.

[167]

"I guess it's blown over," he fretted for the hundredth time. "If we were going we'd know by now." For days he scarcely left his study, and when he did he called back from every stop.

"Any message?" he would ask.

On Saturday, at three o'clock, a Western Union boy pedaled up to the house, and father met him on the porch.

"Get your lightning rod up, Bill," an enigmatic telegram read, "lightning is about to strike."

Father laughed aloud, hurried to his study, and took out a sermon he had written months before and was saving for a special day. Next morning he entered his pulpit eagerly, dressed in his careful best. He began the service with particular dignity, but while the choir was singing the anthem, just before the Scripture reading, he crossed his knees, and his left leg began to bob up and down. His eyes directed mother's glance to the aisle where four men, all strangers, had slipped into an inconspicuous pew.

Completely at ease, father arose and preached one of the best sermons of his life, a rational interpretation of the miracles.

He pointed out that the Oriental mind translates everything into figures of speech. He explained how, in *The Arabian Nights*, the genii who rose from the sea were the voices of conscience, or obstacles in the path of the hero. The man who slew countless dragons was overcoming the daily problems of life. The Oriental merely made his commonplace existence more exciting by dramatizing it.

Then he turned to the Bible, calling attention to its many Oriental expressions. He interpreted Moses' fast of forty days and forty nights as a symbol for the longest length of time man could endure a trial, just as today a mother, reminding her son that she has told him "a million times" to wash his hands, speaks not literally but forcefully.

With this foundation, father explained that Jesus, understanding the imaginative quality of His listeners' mentality, often spoke in parables. He pointed out that the Bible should be read with this fact in mind and elaborated Jesus' own explanation of the parables in the eleventh and twelfth verses of the fourth chapter of Mark: "Unto you is given the mystery of the kingdom of God; but unto them that are without, all things are done in parables; that seeing they may see, and not perceive; and hearing they may hear, and not understand."

It was a sermon to impress college professors.

Afterward father greeted the strangers as though he was unaware they were delegates (the "lightning") from Morningside. He welcomed and captivated them with his personality. Quite by accident, mother, Eileen, Fraser, and I appeared in the vestibule and were introduced. There was not a flaw anywhere.

A few days later the bishop informed father that Morningside had asked for him. Father pretended surprise.

"Well," he said frankly, "if there was anything I could do here I would gladly stay. But as it is, I am wasting my time."

The bishop agreed.

Within a few weeks father shipped his books and furniture by freight to Morningside, bundled Eileen, Fraser, and me into the rear seat of the Ford, and installed mother beside him in front. Since a large trunk monopolized the rear floor we children rode with our feet higher than our heads for almost two hundred miles.

For a long time father was silent as we rattled out of Omaha, crossed the Missouri River, and turned northward amid rolling bluffs, following the river's winding course through the towns of Missouri Valley and Mondamin. Toward midafternoon we rolled down a long hill to the Missouri valley floor and beheld a great sweep of prairie and cornfields, green and shimmering in the sun. Father smiled.

"This is better!" he exclaimed. "It's beginning to look like home."

A moment later we passed a roadside vegetable stand. Father jumped on the brake, leaped from the car, and returned, carrying a large watermelon.

"At the first brook," he said, "we'll cool this off and have a little snack. We need a little lunch."

And rest we did in a cottonwood grove where there was a splashing stream. Father became talkative as he began to eat.

"You know, Hope, I've been thinking. Why was my ministry in Omaha a failure? Was it the congregation, or was it I?"

Mother weighed her reply carefully and spoke slowly. "I'm not sure. It was our first experience with a city pulpit. There was a great difference in the pace of living. Perhaps it's the war, perhaps it was just the city. I don't know."

Father nodded.

"Oh, it's not the pace I mind. I like speed. It's the difference in values that worries me. I can't reconcile it with what Christianity means to me."

"Yes," mother answered quietly. "I understand, but I have the feeling that deep underneath their values are the same as yours. You just expressed them differently."

She looked across the fields to the twisting, indolent Missouri river.

"It occurs to me," she said, "that sometimes it is important in life to stop for a moment. We are always rushing on, from one church to another, from one building campaign to another, from one problem to another. I think that even though you don't realize it you learned a lesson during those three perfect months in Omaha when you had nothing to do. Your family was happy, even if you weren't."

"Oh, I wasn't unhappy. But what lesson did I learn?"

"Well, take the movies, for example." Mother chose her words painstakingly. "You were very much opposed to them until you saw them in their true light. Now we can all enjoy them. Also, you were bitter that you could not hold a revival service. Could it be that the modern generation just doesn't respond to that type of ministry? Thinking has changed. Perhaps the revival is outmoded."

"In that case, the religious spirit is outmoded, too."

"Not at all. The people of Omaha go to church. But they also play golf and bridge. Their *approach* to Christianity is different from yours—"

"Well," father interrupted, "I like mine better."

"Of course, you do, and so do I. But what approach would win these people? They are still human beings, with weaknesses, heartaches, and longings. You just have to probe deeper to find them, because the outer veneer is thicker."

Father glanced at her sharply. "What you are implying

is that I should overlook their sins and coddle to their weaknesses."

"Oh, no," mother answered. "I mean that when your parish does not agree with your standard you should try to understand and not merely condemn. Do you remember making Samson throw away his cheese because in it was a little wine? Might it not have been better if you had accepted the cheese for what it was—the greatest gift it was in Samson's power to bestow, and he was bestowing it on you?"

"I have always been sorry about that," father admitted. "Then you think I should accept these modern ideas and try to lead people into paths that will do them the least harm?"

"Something like that."

Father nodded. "I see what you mean. Perhaps that's right. Even the Discipline is changed every four years."

Father tossed his melon rind into the stream and turned toward the car. "All right," he called, "let's go."

We drove away again, this time with purposeful speed. But not until we had passed the towns of Sloan and Sergeant Bluff did father speak again.

"Perhaps, mother," he said, "Omaha wasn't such a failure after all."

17

❧

WE STAYED in Morningside more than four years, years that were among the happiest and saddest of father's career.

The people, the city, and the church were ideal for a man of father's temperament. His congregation was composed chiefly of professors and their families, students and professional men from Sioux City. Our family became a part of college life; we attended its parties and athletic events and had access to its lectures and library. Because Morningside was a church college father was a spiritual leader of importance.

Morningside stood on the heights overlooking Sioux City. In the distance, on the bank of the Missouri River, a monument to the Lewis and Clark expedition struck its shaft into the sky, a constant reminder that we were on historic ground.

Up a long, sweeping hill from the river stretched Garretson Avenue—wide, quiet, lined with elms. Halfway up the hill Morningside College took possession of the heights and held them to the summit. And on the fringe of the campus, set deep in an apple and cherry orchard, was the parsonage—a full block from the church.

[173]

A fine house, it was swept in summer by cooling river breezes that rustled the orchard leaves and made us forget the years we had spent in less attractive surroundings.

The great stone church, covered with ivy to the top of the carillon tower, dominated the hilltop and was expansively situated in lawns that swept out into a wide horizon of college buildings. Here was a real house of worship, as handsome as that father had built in Fort Dodge, and along the same architectural lines: a large auditorium with a clear view of the pulpit from the last rows of the balcony, a separate wing for the Sunday school, a dry basement with a well-equipped kitchen, and a large organ and choir loft.

With this Utopia to work in, father logically expected a miserable choir and abominable music, for no church is perfect. But the organist was head of the college music department, and the singers were a college group directed by the school's vocal teacher, Mr. McCollom.

Even before we had settled our new home father was plunged into his ministry. On the day we arrived Horace Knight, the Sunday-school superintendent, died of pneumonia, leaving a wife and three small children. Knight had gone duck hunting and had stood all day at the river's edge in a raw rain. Three days later he was dead.

Father hurried to Mrs. Knight and found her hysterical, surrounded by helpless children and neighbors. Quietly father asked to be left alone with her.

"I am your pastor, Mrs. Knight," he said. "Isn't there something I can do for you?"

"Nothing," she sobbed.

"I know it is difficult for you to receive a total stranger in such a tragic hour, but won't you try to think of me as a friend you have known as long as you have known your church?'"

Mrs. Knight did not respond.

"No words I might say can bring back your husband," father continued gently. "But you can take consolation. He has gone to join his God. Much as you are heartbroken at losing him, try to think of the glory that has come to him."

This only brought on a new fit of weeping. Father let her cry. When the grief-assuaging sobs subsided he spoke again.

"Perhaps a prayer would help you."

Mrs. Knight rose, her face distorted. "Oh, go away, please," she begged. "I don't *want* to pray. I'll never pray as long as I live."

Father looked at her compassionately. "Ah, yes," he said simply, "but you will. When the pain is less sharp you will pray again. You will find Jesus a great comfort in your loneliness."

"No, never," the widow cried. "Why did He have to take Horace away? God had the whole world to choose from. Why did He take Horace, when *we* need him so much? *I hate God.*"

She threw herself down on a sofa. Sadly father went to her, sat down, and put his arm around her.

"I know, but have you stopped to think that *God* may be disappointed, too? I have no doubt God had a great work cut out for Horace in this world. Otherwise he would not have given him such a brave wife and such dear children. But it is not God's fault that Horace stood in a duck blind in the rain until he caught pneumonia. He cannot be responsible for the carelessness of His children. Believe me, God is weeping *with* you today. You are no more grieved than He."

He left her then to meditate on what he had said. And when, next day, he buried Horace Knight, the widow knelt at the grave to pray.

The sudden loss of a jovial active church member such as Horace Knight cut deeply into a congregation already unnerved by the increasing prospect of America's entry into the war. President Wilson had just been re-elected on the slogan "He kept us out of war," but no one was deceived. Military engineers already had selected part of Morningside campus as a site for buildings to house a student army training corps.

There were at least one hundred and fifty young men in the congregation eligible for war service. A few hotheads already had gone overseas with Canadian troops and one by one had been killed in battle. Father's sermons preached faith, but each Sunday he had more difficulty in dissipating the general gloom. Something must be done.

"I'll have to find a way to cheer them up," he told mother after an unusually depressing December Sunday. "Otherwise this will be the unhappiest Christmas of their lives."

All week he deliberated. By Saturday he knew what to do.

"Don't be alarmed if you hear a joke from the pulpit, Hope," he advised. "It will be only a gentle one. But I must get them laughing somehow, even in church."

The next morning he spoke of the sacrament of Baptism and what it meant to Christians. Into his discourse he injected these words: "A mother once asked me if it was right to baptize a child in the cradle instead of waiting until the child was old enough to understand. I answered, 'Mrs. Lawson, I never knew of a case where infant baptism harmed a child, and it has always had a remarkable effect on the parents.' "

This brought a smile. The following Sunday he told another anecdote. His argument was that sin gets such a hold on a man that he will find any excuse to justify it.

"It's like a tale the old circuit riders tell," he said. "A preacher went to Conference, and the elders were examining his character. The charge was made that Brother Hawley never converted anybody. One of the preachers asked, 'Does he make anybody mad?'

" 'Oh, no,' the elder replied, 'he's a very lovable character.'

" 'Well,' the preacher snapped, 'if he can't convert anybody and can't make anybody mad, I'm opposed to him.' "

A murmur of laughter rippled through the church. From that day on father conducted a conscientious campaign of cheer. He ordered a new set of books from the Methodist Book Concern called *Wit and Humor of America* and began diligently to read and quote from Mark Twain.

Quite by accident he learned that one of his parishioners, a retired farmer named Casper Cullenbaugh, had a very contagious laugh. He made the discovery on Wednesday night at a parish supper. While waiting for the crowd to be seated, he found himself beside Cullenbaugh and by way of conversation recounted an episode in his early ministry. He had gone to the country to attend a sick woman and had been met by a pugnacious Irish terrier. The dog chased father into a pasture.

At this point Cullenbaugh began to laugh. Father decided to polish the tale by putting into the pasture a bellicose Black Angus bull. Father decided to jump a barbed-wire fence rather than try to convert the bull. But it seemed preachers were anathema to the fence, too for, as father sailed over, the fence reached up and relieved him of some vital clothing.

Cullenbaugh began to yip in a high-pitched, uncontrollable good humor. As the episode unfolded he held his sides. He leaned over backward and doubled up nearly to the floor. Other church members looked in his direction and began to smile.

Quick to sense the value of this mirth, father knuckled down and gave his story everything he had. After jumping the fence, he discovered that the dog had returned with re-enforcements. The new dogs, too, pursued him down the road, tearing off more of his clothes. But father was a fast runner and soon winded the dogs. They sought more allies. Their barks brought a mighty response from neighboring farms. Soon the dogs' brothers and sisters were on father's trail, then their cousins and nephews, then their aunts and stepchildren, and finally their grandmothers, and great-grandsires by marriage once removed.

Cullenbaugh howled. His body shook all over, letting go a trail of laughter. All over the room people had stopped eating. Father knew that they were watching, first curiously, then humorously. At last they, too, began to laugh. Father laughed. And still his story grew.

Inside a quarter mile the dogs had deprived him of all his clothes except his long underwear, his collar, and his shoes. Cullenbaugh's eyes were in tears.

Finally, when every dog in the county was chasing him

and sampling his exposed flesh, father decided Cullenbaugh had had enough. With the Irish terriers snapping behind, he crossed the county line, to discover that he had emerged from an Irish community into one infested with Orangemen, whose dogs hated Irish terriers more than the terriers hated father. So from far and wide the Orangemen's dogs descended on the Irish, and in the excitement father escaped.

Next day everyone in the church was chuckling over the way father had discovered Cullenbaugh's infectious yipping laughter and had gone to work on it. The dog yarn was told and retold until people almost forgot the impending war.

Thereafter, for the duration of the war, father hunted up a good Sunday laugh for Casper Cullenbaugh. Casper was lame and sat at the back of the church; hence he was first to reach the vestibule where father always shook hands with everyone. Father stopped him at the door and told him a story. Casper never before had been in the limelight, and he loved it. Long before the climax of the story he would start to yip, and by the time father's narration ended everyone in the church was in a jovial humor.

The people learned to expect this byplay. They would linger inside the church until the yipping began, then look at one another and smile.

"There goes Mr. Spence," they would say, "making Casper laugh again."

Where father got all his stories I don't know, nor does mother. Undoubtedly he dug some from old-time books in the college library. Some he invented.

One, probably adapted from a joke book, was this:

An old-time revivalist was preaching one night in a particularly tough neighborhood. Several times in this town he had been interrupted by raucous interpolations from the congregation. This night he was going strong.

"In my ministry," he said, "I have been governed by two spirits. One is the Good Spirit that prompts me to be good and do good. The other is—"

"Whisky," finished a voice from the crowd.

Another story concerned a revival meeting. The preacher had almost finished a discourse on the salvation of the soul when a listener arose and asked, "Brother Jones, how do you know you have a soul?"

"Why, I feel it."

"You can feel it. That means you can touch it."

"No, I didn't mean that."

"Well, can you see it?"

"No."

"Can you smell it?"

"No."

"Can you taste it?"

"No."

"Can you hear it?"

"No."

"Then the senses are against you. You have no soul."

The preacher was not at all abashed.

"Brother Skeptic," he retorted, "did you ever have a toothache?"

"Why, yes."

"Did you touch it?"

"No."

"Did you see it?"

"No."

"Did you smell it?"

"No."

"Did you taste it?"

"No."

"Did you hear it?"

"No."

"Then you never had a toothache," the preacher snapped and continued his sermon.

But there was no humor in father the day the United States entered the war.

He was in the church study when he heard newsboys shouting the terrible news outside his window.

Slowly he climbed the narrow circular stairs to the belfry, reached for the carillon controls, and began to play. As he played he lifted his voice and sang:

> Lead kindly Light, amid th' encircling gloom,
> Lead Thou me on!
> The night is dark, and I am far from home;
> Lead Thou me on!
> Keep Thou my feet; I do not ask to see
> The distant scene; one step enough for me.
>
> So long Thy power hath blest me, sure it still
> Will lead me on.
> O'er moor and fen, o'er crag and torrent, till
> The night is gone,
> And with the morn those angel faces smile,
> Which I have loved long since, and lost awhile!

Thereafter, as long as the war lasted, each night at sundown father went to the belfry and played the chimes for half an hour of vesper devotions.

18

❧❧❧

WITHIN a week of America's war declaration the military machine took over the campus. Barracks sprang up where rolling lawns had been before, the football field trembled under the tramp of men drilling, and the walls of the gymnasium echoed to the exciting music of an army band. In classrooms, study halls, and even in the church students in khaki uniforms predominated.

These manifestations, which made us feel that we were living in a fort rather than in an Iowa town, brought the war closely home to everyone and made father's purpose extremely difficult to achieve.

And he had a purpose, planned long in advance: to prevent hysteria and to make sure that, in the chaos of war, God was not forgotten.

The four New Testament Gospels became his Bible, and in them he found texts for sermons of strength and courage: but he did not preach on the fifth chapter of Matthew, 44: "Love thy enemies." He continued to lighten his sermons with bright anecdotes, so that sometimes it was difficult to tell whether he was preaching or delivering an after-dinner address.

When people came to him heavy-laden, he began immediately to joke about anything that came into his mind. Scores left his presence laughing so heartily that they did not realize that, without even unburdening themselves, their troubles had been dissipated. Others were convinced that, in comparison with the world at large, they had nothing to worry about.

But even the parsonage could not escape the war. The Red Cross flag hung in our window. My coat glittered with pins and buttons proving our participation in Liberty Loan and War Savings Stamp drives. Prices soared, and with each rise father's salary seemed to shrink. Mother went back to baking bread, which we "buttered" with margarine.

When the army barracks finally were completed father called on Major Patrick, commander of the cantonment.

"I'm Mr. Spence," he introduced himself, "and I'd like a job as chaplain to this outfit."

"All right," said the major, looking up from his papers, "make yourself at home."

Father did. In two weeks he knew everybody by his full name, but not once did he try to convert the lads or exhort them to make their peace with God lest they be killed in battle. Instead, he helped them write letters home, straightened out their thinking on problems in calculus and chemistry, and wrote their English essays. He was a companion and hoped his example would lead them to respect his way of life.

"If they live as Christians," he told President Mossman one day, "they have nothing to fear—here or elsewhere."

All he wanted from them was respect. He received it from all but one group—a dozen or more young men who

had not been on the campus before the war. They resented him. They played cards conspicuously when he visited the dormitories. When, at taps, he stood beside the bugler and quietly spoke the words: "Bless these Thy children, O God, and give them peaceful rest," they raised their voices loudly. Father tried to combat this by inviting the ringleaders to the parsonage; they declined.

He went out of his way to be helpful, without avail. If he joined their baseball game they stopped playing.

One day he came upon six of them shooting craps. He stood by until he saw how the game was played, then sat down among them.

They were expecting a moral lecture. To head it off, one lad defiantly tossed him the dice.

"Try it, Parson, it will do you good."

Father calmly took the dice, blew on them, and shook them. The boys were surprised; their idea of a chaplain was a stiff-backed soul saver. But, since they still anticipated a lecture on the evils of gambling, they decided to have their fun first.

"Two bits you don't make your point," one challenged, tossing out a quarter.

"All right," father responded, and threw. To everyone's surprise, up turned a winning four and three.

"Well, I'll be damned!" his opponent exclaimed, and then, realizing what he had said, awaited the castigation he was sure would follow. But father desired only to be accepted, not to reform.

"That is Hell, isn't it?" he remarked tactfully and walked away.

The boys were stunned. One recovered sufficiently to call, "Say, Chaplain, you forgot your winnings."

Father turned, delighted at this indication of fellowship.

"I can't accept it," he called back, "I didn't have a quarter in my own pocket to pay if I had lost."

From then on he was chaplain in fact as well as name.

Crapshooting and card games continued, of course, but were less popular after father introduced lawn bowling and curling. He even taught the student soldiers cricket so that when they arrived overseas they would have a team ready for the British. And when profanity arose in the excitement of a contest he ignored it.

Once he even complimented it. Louis d'Angeli, a member of the corps who had come out of the Sioux City stockyards, struck out in a crucial moment of a baseball game. He curled the corners of home plate with sizzling oaths, then saw father.

"Louis," father said, "when a man can cuss for two minutes and twenty seconds without repeating himself once, it's an art!"

By the beginning of May father was so much an institution in the training corps that one of the Sioux City papers wrote an article about him. A few days later a Y.M.C.A. executive from Chicago, whom father had known for years, appeared at the parsonage.

"Bill," he announced before he was inside the front door, "I want you to take a Y unit to France."

Father caught his breath. "What makes you think I could do that, Jeff?" he asked.

"Everyone knows the work you have done on the campus," Jeff Nichols replied, "and we desperately need men over there with your leadership and courage."

For once father did not make a quick decision. When he consulted mother, she said: "This is one time, Will, when I cannot help you. We have tackled everything together for a long time, but in this you must do as *you* think best."

She refused to discuss the matter. Father, who was helpless if he could not talk out loud to someone, went to Dr. McKaig, a retired Methodist circuit rider.

[186]

/ "Bob," father began, "I've been invited to take a Y unit to France. You've been a practical parson for sixty years. What do you think of my going?"

"Don't do it," Dr. McKaig answered shortly. The Scotsman never wasted words.

"Is that all you have to say?"

"Yes."

"Don't you even want to discuss it?" father asked.

"No."

"You won't hear my reasons why I think I should go?"

"No."

"Why?"

"Because you're an idiot."

"Why?"

"I was through the Civil War," Dr. McKaig answered. thoughtfully stroking his white Vandyke, "and I know what war is like. The energy of the whole nation is concentrated on hate and slaughter, and a preacher's place is at home counteracting the damage."

"But a pastor is also needed to attend the dying in the field."

"True, but even that is not as important as something else. When a war ends the reconstruction period is as terrible as was the conflict. I saw what happened in '65. Men who have been at war don't come home and settle back into their previous existence as though nothing had happened. They're used to the barbaric rule of kill or be killed, and *after* this war the influence of Christ really will be needed. Instead of going away, it is your Christian duty to prepare yourself and your congregation for that day."

Father tried to argue the point but failed.

[187]

All over town he went, searching for someone who would tell him his duty lay overseas. He wanted desperately to go. But no one would encourage him.

June came, and Morningside college graduated sixty-nine men into the army, eleven into Y.M.C.A. service, and three into the Methodist ministry. Father was responsible for the last three.

Graduation day brought home, as had nothing previously, the personal tragedy of war. With so many young men marching off to war father became too busy even to think of going himself. And in another few months circumstances forced him to discard the idea entirely.

The influenza epidemic descended upon the community. Father was called to the bedside of many of his members and scores of strangers. In the presence of death people summon a preacher even though they have never been in a church. Father also called at four hospitals as often as three times a day to visit parishioners or patients from farms and rural settlements who were far from friends and spiritual advisors. The hospital authorities telephoned him many a night to come and administer the sacrament to a man or woman whose name he did not know.

Shortly after three o'clock one morning the mother superior at a Catholic hospital asked him to hurry over. He found a woman dying of influenza, and her newborn daughter almost dead.

"I think you can do something for them," the mother superior said. "They are not Catholics, and the mother is too weak to talk."

Father went to their room. The dying mother smiled

faintly, and he administered the sacrament to her. But she kept looking at her baby.

The mother superior picked up the child and looked at father. "I think she should be baptized."

"What is her name?"

"I don't know. We never found out."

"What shall we call her?" father asked, preparing for the ritual.

The mother superior thought a moment and smiled. "Let's call her Mary," she replied. "It's a good enough name for any child."

Father nodded. "Mary," he said, "I baptize thee in the name of the Father and of the Son and of the Holy Spirit, Amen."

"Amen," the sister whispered.

A few minutes later both mother and child were dead.

These and other experiences, particularly funerals, noticeably aged father. In one day, at the height of the epidemic, there were seven funerals. He was even compelled to forget his rule against burial on the Sabbath. One Sunday morning he was half an hour late for service because he could not leave a bedside. Finally he dispensed with the morning service altogether and announced that he or Dr. McKaig would be in the church every afternoon and evening to conduct brief prayer meetings.

Funerals made father physically ill. He could withstand any pain and face death itself, but he hated funerals. Time and again he walked the street for an hour getting up courage enough to go to one. He so loved every member of his flock that an interment was a personal grief, all the harder to bear because he could not reveal his own emotion. More than once he returned from the cemetery with his clothes soaked with perspiration, so exhausted that he collapsed as soon as he entered the house.

At the peak of the epidemic a lad of sixteen died. The boy had attended Sunday school, but his father, a greens-keeper at a golf club, did not go to church.

Father went to the shabby home as soon as he learned of Howard Carson's death. Late at night he stumbled up a boardwalk, sidestepping a belligerent dog, and knocked. Howard's father opened the door.

"What do you want?" he asked in a surly, suspicious voice.

"I just heard," father faltered, "that you have lost Howard. I came to offer what help I can."

Carson's expression changed from one of defense almost to one of relief when he learned his caller was the minister. But the relief quickly disappeared, and in its stead came anger.

"Get out," he shouted, "or I'll put the dogs on you. I don't want any praying around here!"

"All right," father said, "I won't pray. But is no one with you? I was Howard's friend. He might like to know that I called."

"You can't do him any good now. So get out!" He slammed the door in father's face.

The next day father returned and in a trying interview finally gained consent to give Howard a Christian burial. The funeral service was held in an undertaker's chapel, with a few of the boys in Howard's Sunday-school class serving as pallbearers. Father had personally asked them to help. Mr. Carson did not appear at the chapel, but was in the cemetery when the cortege arrived. Although two more funerals awaited him, father took particular pains to see Howard respectfully to the grave, but he was obliged to abbreviate the ritual.

" 'I am the resurrection and the life,' " he began; " 'he that believeth in Me, though he were dead, yet shall he live; and whosoever liveth and believeth in Me shall never die.' Unto Thee we now entrust the spirit of this youth, knowing that in Thy love he will find eternal peace."

Just as the words were concluded two men stepped forward brusquely and clamped handcuffs on Howard's father.

"I have a warrant for your arrest," one of them said. "You are charged with the murder of—" and he named a member of the golf club where Carson worked.

Carson was led away. The few mourners at the grave turned and curiously followed the police. Father was left alone by the casket.

Tears came to his eyes, and he bit his lips. "It's all right, Howard," he said, weeping now. "I will act as your father."

After watching the coffin descend slowly out of sight, he looked aloft into the burning midsummer sky. "Into Thy keeping, O Father," he prayed, "I entrust these, the mortal remains of my son. He was a good boy, Father, be merciful to him."

He stooped, picked up a clod of dirt, and dropped it into the grave. Then slowly he walked to his car and drove to the undertaker's parlor for another funeral.

As the epidemic waned, the newspaper lists of war casualties began to lengthen. Church services were resumed, and almost every Sunday father read out from the pulpit the name of a young man who, the previous year, had attended Morningside college and now was dead.

In both parish and pulpit father was a mighty pillar of confidence and strength. When his work was done, however, he became moody. He was ill from overwork but would not admit it. He began to sit on the porch at dusk, watching the sun sink beyond the river. Then, turning up his coat collar against the dew-laden evening breeze, he would meditate in the dark for hours at a time. This worried mother, and finally she asked if it was necessary.

"The faces of my young men come to me in the dark," he said. "One by one I see them, even though they lie dead in France, and I ask God to give them happiness and peace. I think I will stay out here a little longer. I don't want to overlook anyone."

One November night, after the first snowfall of the season, he retired very late. I heard him plod slowly up the stairs and open the door to his room. Then all was quiet again, and I dropped off to sleep. Some time later Fraser, who shared the bedroom with me, tugged at my sleeve.

"Hartzell, what's that?" he was demanding in alarm, "What's that noise?"

I awakened to the sound of factory-whistle blasts, insistently repeated.

The noise drew nearer. It had started in the depths of industrial Sioux City and had spread out like a heavy fog across the flats. Now it was climbing the long hill to the campus and approaching the church and parsonage. Automobile horns honked ceaselessly, and cowbells were being rung in frenzy. Fraser and I were too frightened to move. Many minutes passed, during which the racket increased relentlessly.

Next we heard footsteps before the house and a call: "Oh, Mr. Spence, come out and ring the chimes."

A moment later it was repeated. Soon it became a chant, punctuated by whoops, cheers, and hoarse shouts that at last we identified: "The war is over! Mr. Spence, come out and ring the chimes!"

Fraser crept into my bed. The door of father's room opened. We heard him walk in slippered feet to Eileen's door, enter, and fling open her window.

"What is it?" he called.

"The war is over! Come out and ring the chimes!"

The window closed. Father descended the stairs, and the front door opened. Fraser and I ran to join mother at Eileen's window. Father stood in the driveway below us, bareheaded in the clear, cold moonlight, his dressing robe drawn closely around him. He gestured for silence.

"It has come at last?"

Joyful shouts convinced him.

Again he lifted his hands, as in a benediction, and everyone became quiet.

"This is no time," he said calmly, "for riotous celebration or ringing of bells. This is a time to give thanks to our Heavenly Father who has granted us this mercy. Let us pray."

He knelt in the snow. One by one the crowd dropped to their knees.

"Almighty God," he prayed, "we thank Thee for Thy blessing that this war has ceased. We thank Thee for Thy gift of courage, which alone has carried us through

[193]

anxious days. We thank Thee for giving us hope that once again we may be privileged to live Christian lives in a warless world. We ask Thy blessing on those who will not again return to live among us. And we beseech Thee, Oh Father, that war may never come again to us, or to our children. Help us to live as brothers in Christ Jesus, that wars may be no more. Give us strength to endure the sorrows of this hour, courage to face the future, when our men come not home, courage to start life anew. And in the troubled days ahead when we are entering what must be a new world, give us *Thy* peace. Amen."

He arose and returned to the house. Slowly the group broke up.

19

❧

NORTH Iowa did not settle down for three years, and during this time father had reason to remember Dr. McKaig's prophesy about the postwar period. He became increasingly thankful that he had not gone overseas. He helped many to make their adjustment; a few he could not assist.

Into his study one blizzardy night in January staggered a derelict in civilian clothes, except for an overseas cap.

Father recognized him as a grocer who had volunteered early.

"Well, Frank Simmons," he exclaimed, "welcome home!"

The soldier did not answer. He went directly to the hot-air register, where he stood warming his feet and hands. Slowly father coaxed him to a chair and waited patiently. Men like Frank Simmons came to him only when moved by unbearable trouble. At last the visitor spoke.

"I came home today from a year in Hell," he said, and the memory of it froze him again into a long silence. "I was discharged at Camp Dodge and came home. But I guess I was a little early. My wife read in the paper that we weren't being dismissed until next week. She wasn't expecting me."

He looked at father with an expression that disclosed his tragedy more plainly than words.

"What am I going to do, Mr. Spence?" he asked helplessly.

"You are going back to your store, Frank," father answered, "and work hard—so hard you'll forget."

Simmons shook his head. "The store is gone."

"Oh, that can't be, Frank. It has been doing a fine business."

"She and—Charlie Piper have just sold it. You see, I deeded it to her before I left. They're using the money to go to California. They expected to be gone before I arrived."

Simmons looked aimlessly at his cap, then arose slowly.

Father took his arm and tried to seat him again, but Simmons backed away. "Going to California," he repeated.

"You must be mistaken, Frank," father said. "Ethel wouldn't do a thing like that. You've just become confused in the excitement of returning home. Stay with us tonight. Things will look different in the morning."

"No, no," Simmons declined quickly, "thanks, Pastor. A man comes home from the war, but it—it isn't home any more."

Despite father's entreaties, he stumbled away into the blizzard.

Father knew that time would effect its own cure among most of the adults and that his work was done when he had taught them patience. But he was deeply worried about the children of fifteen and sixteen who were going to public dance halls, smoking cigarettes, and giving bridge parties. He was baffled by his inability to reach the young. He could not do it through the church, because they never came to church. Their parents took them on Sunday outings or into the country to see a farm in which they were interested. Everyone was buying farm land. Fabulous profits were turned overnight. Farmers and city folk alike mortgaged their future to buy more and more land and, eventually, oil stocks. Father did not preach against this moral breakdown, nor did it particularly concern him. But an occasional incident frightened him regarding the future.

A girl of good family had come to the college from a little town near by and regularly attended both church and Epworth League. She was pretty, serious, and studious. One day she telephoned father for an appointment and told him she had been seduced under promise of marriage, only to discover that her lover already had a wife and family.

Father's instinct was to horsewhip the man, but he calmed down when he realized that the girl was in serious trouble that might ruin her life. Quietly he let it be known that she was going away for "summer study at Chicago University" and arranged for her admission to a Florence Crittenden home. When she returned to Morningside in the fall her baby had been adopted.

With the reopening of school in the autumn in 1919, father and mother redoubled their efforts to interest young people in the church. Father chose to work among the high school and college students. Mother became active with the intermediate department of the Sunday school and the Junior League.

The latter was not the nationally known society organization. In fact, once mother became very indignant when she discovered that some debutantes whose pictures appeared in the newspapers were not active in the church.

"Aren't these girls a little old to be still in the Junior League?" she asked one day, holding up her paper for father to see.

He laughed. "Not *that* one, mother," he replied. "But don't worry about it. I doubt if they ever heard of *your* Junior League, either."

Mother, of course, was referring to a part of the Epworth League, named for the town in England where John Wesley was born. The Epworthians were young people from sixteen to twenty years old, and the Junior League started at the age of ten or eleven and graduated its members into the more adult society.

Sunday school met in the morning and the Junior League at half-past six Sunday evening. Mother became engrossed in them, but not merely because she was a preacher's wife. She always chose work she liked. In a church that had only 350 youngsters of intermediate-department age, mother built a Sunday school of nearly 500. She took a special interest in the children of non-church families, creating tasks for them, giving them responsibilities, and sharing the intimacy of parsonage life with them by letting them help her prepare Sunday's work. Most of them later joined the church.

Her most vexing problem concerned the daughters of two Morningside professors. The men were rivals, their wives competed socially, and the girls naturally assimilated the attitude. Previous Sunday-school leaders had sidestepped the issue by dividing the class the two children should have shared. Thus, because the girls could not get along together, two teachers became necessary.

Mother decided that this feud was not Christian. She reunited the classes and told the girls they must get along.

They went home and reported. The next day a militant mother walked up the parsonage steps and rang the bell with a violence that brought father from his study and mother from her sewing.

"Oh, oh," father whispered, peeping out the window, "it's Mrs. Elder. You're in for it now." He crept back to his study, but left his door ajar.

Mother cordially invited her guest into the living room and began to talk as though Mrs. Elder merely was paying a social call. She kept the conversation spinning so fast that Mrs. Elder departed without mentioning her complaint.

As soon as she had gone father popped from the study, laughing heartily. "Beautiful," he exclaimed, "beautiful!" He went around chuckling all day.

The professors' daughters remained in one class and even came to like each other in time.

Mother taught in Sunday school, but in the Junior League she merely guided. The League in the Methodist church, like the Christian Endeavor and Young People's society in other churches, introduces children to active participation in religious affairs. They learn to discuss the Scriptures, to pray aloud in a group, and to decide for themselves what, in their own lives, shall constitute a Christian example.

Father was usually unable to attend the Junior League

service because of another group meeting at that hour. But one night his curiosity became so strong that he tiptoed to the church basement to see how mother was getting along. Not only was she doing remarkably well, but his own daughter was playing the piano and a son was leading the singing.

With a start he realized that his children had begun to grow up. The next day, when he saw Eileen in his library, he paused to ask what book she was reading. It was *Jane Eyre*.

"Where did you get that?" he asked.

"From the bookcase."

"Do you like it?"

"Very much."

Father was as pleased as though he had just received a ten-dollar wedding fee. He was immensely proud of his library. In it was every standard reference of any value, a great many biographies and novels, complete sets of history, philosophy, medical texts, and even a few rare first editions. He bought every book he could afford and many he could not. Always remembering how lonely his library had looked in the vast shelves at Laketon, he never threw away a book. Every time a deceased parishioner's library was liquidated father begged a few volumes from the heirs. In twenty years he accumulated a literary collection that, together with the big sectional bookcases to house it and his library furniture, once required an entire freight car to move. He often boasted that his children need never go to the public library for assistance in their schooling.

Before long he also discovered that Eileen played the piano well, and he began to sit in the living room while she practiced Chopin etudes. He even reorganized his work schedule to hear her in a recital. She was to play Schubert's "Hark, Hark the Lark."

Nervous because father was in the audience, Eileen began at too fast a tempo. Finding that she could not sustain it at the octaves, she stopped playing, then tearfully corrected her tempo, and finished the number. In the eyes of her teacher she was disgraced, but father was happy.

"You did very well," he complimented her afterward, "very well. You needn't cry about accelerating that tempo. I heard Paderewski do it in concert once—on that very piece. And, besides, the important thing is that you corrected your mistake and carried on. It's not hard to make a mistake, but it is mighty difficult to *admit* one in public. I don't know ten people in the world with that much courage."

Eileen rallied immediately.

Having publicly admired one child, he next went to hear me in a school declamation. My oration was *The Flagmakers*, by Franklin K. Lane. Father at first did not believe the judges' announcement of the winner. He turned toward me, amazed that he had a son old enough for any accomplishment.

"You!" he gasped incredulously.

Going home, he asked mother if she realized that in five years her daughter would be in college and two years later her older son.

Less than a month after this he was organizing a drive to raise a half-million-dollar endowment for Morningside College. Up and down North Iowa he stumped, exhorting preachers to cooperate and cornering wealthy laymen for donations. Many a dollar of speculative capital went directly from the pocket of the profiteer to father's hand for Morningside. He could spot money a hundred miles away and went after it. But, true to his custom of not asking from others what he himself would not do, he pledged five hundred dollars, the utmost he could give.

In six months the endowment goal was crossed, and father became, indeed, a personage on the campus. Every professor who otherwise would have lost his chair because of the lean period that had hit the college when Federal aid was cut off after the war, and every proud alumnus was his friend.

It was natural that he was asked, in the spring of 1920, to give the graduation address. He had delivered scores of these to high school graduates, but this was to be his first college commencement, and he decided to make it memorable.

He spoke directly to the graduates in their own breezy vernacular, not caring very much whether their elders understood him or not. He pointed out that in a chaotic world stability and nobility of character were youth's greatest assets.

Previously the custom had been a flowery sixty-minute oration that said nothing. His listeners were amazed and delighted at father's hard hitting, down-to-earth discourse. They listened. And they cheered when suddenly he pocketed his watch and said, "Well, I've talked ten minutes, and that's enough. You are all anxious to get started in life, and there's no use my delaying you. I've only one piece of advice to give you about life: never grab a bull by the tail unless you know his first name and his family connections."

President Mossman was embarrassed. He had prepared a surprise for the occasion, and now he had to restore enough dignity to carry it off. Somehow it didn't seem right to give a Doctor of Divinity degree to a man who had been talking about bulls' tails.

But he managed adroitly. "No man," he said, "is more qualified than you are, Brother Spence, to give us that advice. Time after time I've watched breathlessly while you tackled an almost impossible job, and every time you carried it through."

Father smiled.

"The words you have spoken here," Dr. Mossman went on, "prove your greatness. You have couched your message in the very language of this world none of us is quite sure about."

Everyone laughed.

"But there is a universal language that applies to you: the language of respect. For seventeen years you have been a tower of faith in teaching Christianity. You have taught it by living it, until your leadership is unchallenged throughout the state."

He took up a box that had been hidden behind his chair, opened it, and brought forth the red hood of the Doctorate of Divinity.

"In recognition of your service to Christ and to man, it is my privilege, on behalf of Morningside college, to bestow upon you this hood, Dr. Spence."

He placed the mantle on father's shoulders.

On the way home father unrolled the parchment that had accompanied the degree, read it, and gasped. "Mother," he said, "look at this!"

The scroll was inscribed to Gulielmus Henricus Spence.

"Where the mischief do you suppose they ever got that name Henry?"

He gazed at it critically and then laughed.

"A half-million-dollar endowment, five hundred of it from my own pocket—and they go and call me Henry!"

But he was proud. For the first time in his life he had a middle name.

20

❦

FATHER often said that, like Paul, the preacher has no continuing city. And as soon as the church and people of Morningside were serene again he began looking for a new world to conquer.

In October, 1921, we drove to Denver, Colo., in our Model T Ford. Over Nebraska's gravel roads we bounced, accompanied by herds of tumbleweed, which were uprooted by the wind and rolled in clusters so thick that sometimes the prairie itself seemed to be in motion.

The second night we spent at McCook, Neb. When we awoke the sun was beating down with the heat of midsummer. Ahead lay a journey across such burning and almost deserted flats that even father's optimism sagged. To keep us children quiet he explained how we were traversing a gently rising plain that would lead us eventually onto a plateau a mile high.

"I'll give a dollar," he promised, "to the child who first sees the mountains."

He had no trouble with us that day. We strained our eyes westward, trying to spot something we had never seen, deceived time and again by puffs of clouds and occasional insignificant hills. But at last, at about two o'clock, Fraser jumped up with a mighty shout. "I spy!" he exclaimed. "Pay me!"

And he was right. Eileen and I had been so intent on the horizon directly ahead that we had missed a white-capped range to the northwest. Large and larger the mountains grew, taking individual shape at last as we neared Denver.

To children of the prairies this was splendor indeed. But even more exciting was our new home. The ever-rising plain broke sharply within ten miles of a range of foothills and pitched down suddenly to the floor of Cherry Creek. Denver lay in the valley, but before we reached the city we arrived at the suburb of Park Hill, on the rim of the plain overlooking Denver's rooftops. Park Hill church was father's new mission.

He pulled up in front of the parsonage and stepped briskly to the front porch, which commanded a view of great Mount Evans, its peak buried in a crimson sky. Awed by such grandeur, father removed his hat, absorbed the vista in silence for a moment, then quoted: "Lo, He that formeth the mountains and createst the winds, and walketh upon the high places of the earth: the Lord is His name."

Mother was more immediately interested in whether or not her new house was clean. She stepped in the front door and almost bumped into a tall, handsome woman who was trying to tiptoe out without being seen.

"You must be Mrs. Spence," she said when dis-covered. "I'm Mrs. Cook. I just came over to see that everything was spick-and-span. But I didn't want you to catch me in a house dress!"

[206]

"Oh, this is wonderful!" mother sighed, after a quick survey. The floors glistened with a new coat of wax. A new white gas range brightened the kitchen. "I never entered so clean a house."

Mrs. Cook, still embarrassed, followed mother to the back porch.

"That's fine," she said. "But I hope you'll remember the appearance of the house and forget how *I* looked. And I'm *not* going to meet my pastor in this old blue gingham. I'll just run along out the back way."

After her departure father emerged from the dining room, where he had waited tactfully. "Who was that?" he asked.

"Mrs. Cook. She's chairman of the parsonage committee."

"Mrs. Cook," father repeated, intending to remember the name when she returned. From long practice in eating at many tables he had learned to appraise a housewife's culinary skill long before he sampled it. "I'll bet she is a *good* cook, too."

Subsequently he was proved right. She was the best cook in the church.

Park Hill was a new and prosperous suburb into which wealthy Denver merchants and business executives were beginning to move their families. Denver was growing, and because of the mountain barrier it could spread in only one direction: east. The church was in the center of a small community; only seven blocks farther out began a real-estate promoter's dream of thirty-six squares of unimproved streets.

On our arrival the congregation numbered only two

hundred. And the mountains were a constant lure, tempting families away all day Sunday. Winter or summer, the weather was ideal for driving. Even rain was no deterrent. Showers brushed up without warning but lasted only a few minutes. Thus rain on Sunday merely kept home from church those who had not gone on an outing.

Within a month of our arrival mother was active with the intermediates in Sunday school. One morning a threatening storm broke just at the hour of her service, and only twenty children appeared. She faced them bravely.

"I am not going to compliment you," she said, "for coming in the rain. We attend Sunday school to acknowledge our allegiance to Jesus Christ our leader and to worship Him. Instead of being proud that we have come out in bad weather let us be sorry for those who won't be loyal to Him on His own day."

Then she taught them a little verse from her childhood:

> No driving rain can make us stay
> If we have tickets for the play;
> But let one drop the walks besmirch,
> It's far too wet to go to church.

Father's attendance was scarcely larger than hers, and he returned to dinner troubled.

"Mother, why don't we just concede that these people are going to the mountains on Sunday and not fight against their custom? Suppose we hold our service at six in the morning. Then they can all come to church and still have all day in their cottages."

"What," mother reminded him, "about Mrs. Harcourt and Mrs. Beech and all the other older people who don't drive cars? What about the Sunday school?"

Father ate in silence. "Christians," he said firmly, "should sacrifice something for their faith."

"Yes, indeed," mother encouraged him.

"The people of Park Hill don't have to make any financial sacrifices. I think they should prove their love of God is greater than their love of the hills."

"Then you will have to give them real inspiration."

"I'll try, but the competition is pretty stiff. I'll begin by shortening the service."

His sermons continued to be exactly twenty-four minutes long, but he dispensed with announcements altogether, printing them in a bulletin that was distributed by the ushers. Attendance picked up, but throughout his Park Hill pastorate he was surprised if, on an ideally sunny day, his congregation was large.

Father soon came to understand how deeply rooted could be one's love of the mountains. We in the parsonage fell under the spell, too. Father developed the habit of planning a trip into the mountain parks each Saturday. But to do this he had to write his Sunday sermons by Friday night. He sought a short cut in the preparation of his discourses and found one: a twenty-volume set of sermon digests from the works of such illustrious preachers as Dwight L. Moody, Phillips Brooks, and Dr. Talmage. From them he took ideas and texts that would apply to his own needs. Our mountain Saturdays were completely happy for several weeks.

Then one Sunday father was very much depressed when he returned from church.

"Mother," he said at dinner, "that sermon this morning was terrible. I didn't get a single smile out of Mrs. Higgins and not a frown out of Dr. Murphy. Something's wrong."

He wrestled with his problem through two portions of chicken before he discovered the trouble.

"It's those sermon digests," he said. "They've led me into a slovenly habit. I'm not writing sermons any more. I'm cribbing them."

The next day he crated the books and returned them to the publisher.

To father's surprise, the congregation of Park Hill offset its Sunday laxity by turning out abundantly for the midweek meeting.

In other parishes his "prayer meeting" had been a quiet Wednesday night hour with only one or two retired ministers and a few of the older generation who still believed in the "testimonial." He would not even open the church auditorium for such services, preferring to conduct them in a Sunday-school classroom. First came a prayer that he began merely with the words "Let us pray." After a few seconds of silent meditation someone in the audience would ask divine help in a personal problem. Again silence settled over the worshipers, broken by brief pleas: that God comfort a sister who had lost her husband or give strength to a brother in the hospital or open a youngster's eyes that he might see the error of his sinful ways. When father was sure all the individual prayers had been voiced he offered a general supplication of his own. Next he discussed for five minutes some difficult scriptural passage that troubled one of the group. Again there was a period of silence. Then, one by one, each worshiper arose and recited some specific evidence of God's assistance. Thus the prayer meeting was very personal, with the Lord's hand descending directly on those in need. All who attended went away fortified by proof of God's attention to each individual.

The Park Hill midweek was very different. The West was too young for the Methodism of circuit riders. Rather, it had developed a peculiar conglomerate of fun, hospitality, and neighborliness, into which the pastor could weave a little prayer if he desired.

At six o'clock every Wednesday entire families began arriving for a social half hour. By half-past six the Ladies' Aid had supper on the table, charging fifty cents for a dinner worth one dollar and putting aside the collections in anticipation of a subscription they hoped to make to a new building. Wags said later that the new church was decorated on roast beef and lamb stew and carpeted by apple pie. Cooks rivaled each other to produce the best baked beans, the lightest cakes, and the handsomest salads. Father encouraged them.

Sitting at the head of the longest table, he would call clear across the church basement: "Mr. Nelson, can you reach me another piece of Mrs. Leffler's *wonderful* apple pie." If other pies were passed, he would wave them away. "No, Mrs. *Leffler's*, please." No one ever was insulted, however, for if Mrs. Talmadge had brought an apple pie and a pan of rolls father already had whispered in her ear: "I've been trying all through supper to make up my mind whether your rolls or my mother's are the best I ever ate. I've decided for yours."

After the coffee the children went upstairs to meetings

of organizations that fitted their age: for the boys, King's Heralds or Boy Scouts; for the girls, Queen Esthers. The adults remained in the basement to sing a few hymns, listen to father's brief devotions, and then renew their social hour until the children trooped downstairs again promptly at nine o'clock.

Father initiated a church building campaign at one of these suppers. The men were together as at no other time, and one evening after devotions he approached a group of his leaders who were arguing the chances of the University of Denver's football team in a forthcoming game against the University of Colorado.

"Men," he interrupted, "I've news in which you may be interested."

His listeners included Richard Hartington Case, an important lawyer; Stanley Ferris, an extremely shrewd real-estate promoter, and Cass Conway, mining engineer for a New York firm. They stopped their discussion and listened respectfully.

"I had an offer from Baldin-Thomas today of $35,000 for the church property."

"Not bad," Ferris exclaimed, "not bad at all! What do they want it for?"

"They are representing Piggly Wiggly, I think, which wants a store on this corner and would build several floors of apartments overhead."

"Good idea," Ferris admitted. "I wish I'd thought of it."

"When would we have to vacate?" Case asked.

"By the first of the year," father answered.

"But that's impossible," Case pointed out. "I realize we have been thinking about a new church, but we can't sell the roof from over our heads. It will take several years before our plans are complete, you know."

Father had expected that. In every parish there is an unofficial leader of the pastor's opposition. In Park Hill that spokesman was Mr. Case.

"I realize the difficulties," father explained smoothly, "and, of course, any decision is up to the official board. But I don't think we ought to let such a handsome offer slip through our fingers without careful consideration."

"I should say not," Ferris agreed. "This corner isn't worth more than twenty thousand at the outside. We'll never get another chance like this. I say sell it."

"And then what?" Case demanded.

"Then," father went on, "we can use the money to buy a good plot in a growing neighborhood and still have enough left for a nice nest egg when the church is built."

"Very logical," said Case acidly, "but what will we use for worship meanwhile, Mr. Sundlinger's garage?"

Everyone laughed. Ernest Sundlinger owned a beet-sugar refinery and a mushroom farm. He had built a house with a two-car garage the previous year. But Park Hill was far from the schools his four children attended. So he bought each child a car, only to find he had insufficient garaging accommodations. Three times he altered his plans and finally wound up with a garage almost as large as his house.

"Well," father rejoined, "with most of the congregation in the mountains on Sunday, his garage would be almost big enough. But I've a better idea."

"All right, Doctor," Ferris invited, "let's have it. All I ask is a break of twenty-four hours in the location of the

[213]

new building so that I can buy a little property in that neighborhood."

"I propose," father said, "that we sell these premises while we have the chance and buy somewhere else. On a corner of that ground we can erect a temporary tabernacle that will house us until we can plan and build."

Several other men had joined the group by then, and father withdrew, content to let the idea build its own momentum. The rest of the evening the members moved about, discussing the idea in little clusters. By nine o'clock everyone was talking about a location, and Richard Hartington Case was the only one opposed to the sale.

A few weeks later the official board sold the church and bought a full block on the farthest fringe of what then was the residential section. Many persons thought the site too far out. But father repeatedly emphasized the fact that it was on the main automobile boulevard bisecting the suburb.

"In ten years," he said, "we will be in the heart of Park Hill."

Today that prophecy is fulfilled, for the church stands in the center of the community, and the thirty-six blocks that then were vacant lots are solidly set with homes.

The tabernacle was similar to that father had built at Fort Dodge, with two important additions: four tennis courts and a gymnasium. There were a boxing instructor for the boys and a games leader for the girls. Within a year children from nonchurch families were proudly explaining, when they arrived home late for meals, that they had been "over at the church." Their parents, thus interested, soon began attending, too.

After the church suppers, which were continued in the

tabernacle, there were basketball games in the gym. Teams had been organized in every Sunday-school class, and they challenged other Denver church teams to games all winter long.

New arrivals in the community were invited "to come to the tabernacle on Wednesday night and meet your neighbors." The friendliness of everyone was a Christian example that brought new members in by the score. At one Sabbath service, a year after our arrival, father received fifty-six members, most of whom were contacts from the Wednesday suppers.

Sharing so much the pleasures of the church, we children began to drive a wedge between father's personal ideals of conduct and those of the community at large. We bought ice cream on Sunday and joined other children in Sabbath-afternoon sports. But even in following the lead of our neighbors we had to be careful, lest church members object.

Bishop Quayle was asked one time why preachers' children have the reputation of being the least disciplined in town. "Because," he explained, "they have no one to associate with except the children of church members." Actually, parsonage youngsters are unusually straitlaced. No one thinks of objecting if every member of the Sunday-school dances at the American Legion hall, but let the pastor's daughter join them and tongues wag immediately.

One Sunday about six o'clock the telephone rang. A church woman reported to father she had seen me at the theater.

"How did you happen to see him, Mrs. Wright?" father asked.

"Why, he was coming out as I was going in."

"I see," father replied gravely. "I don't think you have any right to criticize the parsonage children for doing something which you do yourself."

He turned thoughtfully from the telephone, and, seeing me, beckoned me into his study.

"I am told you were at a movie today," he began.

"Yes, I was."

"Don't you think that was wrong?"

"No, sir, I don't. I went to church and Sunday school this morning, and I am going to Epworth League tonight. I don't have time to go to the movies during the week, and I don't see any harm in seeing Douglas Fairbanks on Sunday. His shows are always very good."

"Yes," father agreed. "You are old enough now to decide for yourself what is right or wrong. I want you to make up your own mind about such things. But if I were a butcher, you'd help me in the store, even if you didn't like the work, wouldn't you?"

"Yes."

"All right. I am a preacher. You can see that what you did today embarrassed me. You don't want to do that, do you?"

"No, sir."

"Then I hope that as long as you are living at home you will help me with my work."

From then on father's ministry was greatly enhanced by the loyalty of his children. Eileen occasionally rebelled against dictates that limited her wholesome amusement, but she never once let him down in public. Eileen was a sophomore in junior high school. All her friends were dancing. But, tolerant as father was of others' indulgence in this pastime, he denied it to his daughter.

"No child of mine will dance," he said. She could play tennis, explore the hills, and play the piano. But she could neither play bridge nor dance. Of course, she learned both from her girl companions. But none of the boys ever had the pleasure of dancing or card playing with her. And when it came her turn to give a party she invited her friends to dinner and a motion picture. That was as far as she could go.

When Fraser grew older, he, too, showed father scrupulous consideration. In one town our church was only a block from a motion-picture theater. On Sunday night Fraser would not even walk in its direction after the Epworth League service lest someone surmise he was en route to a Sunday show.

Once in a while an act of one of the children that looked particularly black at the moment was of definite value to father. As the Park Hill congregation moved into its tabernacle Richard Hartington Case became more obstinate in his objections to everything that was proposed. Father did his best to win over the lawyer. He played golf with him, invited the Case family to dinner at our house, and appointed Mrs. Case to an important committee. Mr. Case remained, however, behind a stone wall of pomposity. Father believed that if his dignity were once broken down Mr. Case's resistance would diminish.

At that time Fraser was in the beginners' Sunday-school class. A tradition of most churches is Children's Day, when the Sunday school, after weeks of feverish preparation, takes over the morning church service for a day. Father was particular to build this into one of the most important Sundays of the year.

At Park Hill, Children's Day came in May, as a climax

to the Sunday-school year. The objective was to display to the adults the results of a year's religious education. Consequently all the study projects were reviewed, and each department presented an oration, a play, or a tableau. A chorus of young voices, trained by mother, supplanted the choir.

For the beginners, Fraser was chosen to do a little dialogue with a tow-headed youngster named Clarence Gilmore. Their parts were rehearsed carefully. Fraser appeared in a new suit, his first with pants instead of knickerbockers. Clarence was supposed to say the opening line. But he was shy in the presence of so many adults and remained silent. Fraser gave him a cue, but Clarence paid no heed. Fraser nudged, but Clarence merely nudged him in return. Then Fraser twisted Clarence's ear, and Clarence responded not with his own first line, but with Fraser's.

Indignantly Fraser broke out in language not included in the script. "Aw, you nut, that isn't it."

Clarence refused to be humiliated in public. "Who's a nut?" he challenged, and the fight was on.

Their teacher pulled them off the platform amid a roar of applause and laughter.

After the service father, with a wrathful eye, began looking for Fraser.

But he was interrupted by the usually icy Mr. Case, who came up to him, slapped him on the back jovially, and said, "That's *some* son you have, Dr. Spence. It was worth five dollars to me to see that fight. I wish he was *my* boy."

Fraser was saved, and Case became one of father's best friends.

2 1

❧

THE men of Park Hill had definite minds of their own.
Father did not realize that the quick decision to sell the
church on Twenty-third Street and move into a tabernacle on Forest Boulevard was merely a collective
business shrewdness. The men acted promptly to take
advantage of a bargain because they were all in business.
But father misinterpreted their alacrity as proof that he
could lead them where he wanted them to go.

He learned otherwise. In the church father insisted on
being the chief executive. When he gave orders he expected obedience. But almost every male member of his
congregation was also an executive, accustomed to giving
orders and having them obeyed. This stalemated father's
quick judgments.

Everything father proposed of any consequence was
met with the answer, "Let's hold a conference on that."
Then by twos and fours the men would play golf over it,
and mull it over in their minds while driving in the
mountains, and even sometimes submit it to their asso-
ciates downtown for an "outside opinion." Usually weeks
passed before the proper committee met to give the
matter formal consideration.

Exasperated by this conservative procedure, father one night told his official board, "When you press a button downtown everybody jumps; but when I ring nobody jumps."

The women, too, were slow to agree. Nearly everyone had built and furnished a new home within the past year or two. Each, therefore, had definite theories about construction of the church. Some wanted a big parish house and an intimate chapel. Others insisted on a mission-style exterior. Still others demanded a Gothic form. Even those who agreed that there should be a large parish house refused to get together on its shape, facilities, or furnishings. Naturally they discussed these ideas with their husbands. As a group the people of the congregation were wonderful, but separately they were too individualistic to concur on anything.

As Methodists do in cases of disagreement, they began to fight. But their disputes were different from any father had encountered before. The committee members drew on all the tricks of competitive belligerence they found so advantageous in business, and as a result they began to develop permanent grudges.

Eventually it became impossible to get any committee together, because some members would not attend if certain others were present. Meanwhile summer passed, and the new church was not even on the drawing board.

As autumn progressed father's anxiety and frustration increased. Gray hairs appeared, and his temper grew sharp. He had promised to go to Longmont, Colo., forty miles away, and assist at a two-week revival meeting. He dared not think what might happen in his absence.

On the fifth of November, just before he was to leave,

he was advised that the church treasurer, Haynes Potter, and Lane Courtney, the influential owner of a chain of theaters, had stopped playing golf together. Father could not take time to find out the cause of their disagreement, and this worried him.

But during the revival this, with all other extraneous thought, was put out of his mind. Not until he was almost ready to return to Denver did he recall it. Then, almost in a panic, he telephoned mother and asked her to send me to Longmont with as much up-to-date information as possible. I could drive home with him on Sunday night.

I arrived in time for the last Sunday-afternoon meeting. Afterward, as we were walking from the church to the local parsonage, where we were invited for supper, I broke the news that Mrs. Netheridge had resigned from the Monday club.

He was incredulous. "Mrs. Netheridge resigned! Why, she *organized* the Monday club. What's the trouble?"

"She had an argument with Mrs. Ferris."

"With Mrs. Ferris! Great Scott, what about?"

"Mother says Mr. Netheridge and Mr. Ferris had a dispute in the finance committee, and Mrs. Ferris tried to raise the issue with Mrs. Netheridge in front of the whole Monday club. That led to a fight, I guess."

Father began to walk very rapidly, so that I could hardly keep up. "What happened in the finance committee?"

"Well, mother says that Mr. Netheridge agreed with Mr. Potter, and Mr. Ferris said that if Mr. Potter had his way he would resign from the church along with Mr. Courtney."

Father stopped suddenly. "Listen, son," he said, "suppose we start at the beginning. Mother told you this story in logical order, I'm sure. You are starting at the end, not at the beginning. Tell me in mother's words what she said."

I thought diligently. "Oh," I resumed. "Mother said that Mr. Potter wants his bank to lend the church enough money for the building and take a mortgage on the property. Then they won't have to go to all the work of signing up pledges. Mr. Courtney says if they do that he will leave the church, and Mr. Netheridge says he will, too."

"I should think they would," father exploded. "This is the worst yet. Son, we've got to leave for home immediately after the service tonight."

But when we left the church after the evening meeting we discovered that a blizzard had whipped out of the mountains while father was preaching. Snow, lashed by a noisy wind, drove heavily about us. Father's friends urged him not to drive home in the storm, but now he had only one thought: to get back to Denver at the earliest possible moment.

So away we went, the Model T as noisy as the roaring wind. But once out of town we crept in low speed. The snow was so thick we could not see the road ahead. Slowly we felt our way along a winding road through the foothills. We knew the route well, For ten miles it twisted and turned, and at nearly every curve death threatened. Every inch of that first winding ten miles we fought our way.

The wind increased. Sudden gusts blew the car horizontally across the road, into either the cliff or the guard rail. Each time this happened father shouted, "Jump for your life," and we both vaulted from the car without opening the door. Then, laughing at our foolishness, we started off again.

Finally the snow became so thick that the car lights were useless. Father and I took turns driving and guiding. For a half mile I would walk ahead of the car, taking soundings of the road, marking the curves while father drove slowly behind. Then father hiked ahead, and I drove the Ford, my foot jammed constantly on the low-gear pedal. When I became too weary father insisted I rest, and then we scarcely moved along the road.

All the while father was trying to find a solution to this new problem at home, and he grew pessimistic even over our progress. Once the wind, driving from dead ahead, pushed so hard that the car stalled.

"Well, that's the end," he groaned; "we're done for."

I jumped out and began to push, for the grade was sharply downhill. Except for the deep snow the car would have coasted. The engine started again.

A little later the snow lightened, and we could see ten or fifteen feet ahead. I had been the lookout but waited for the car to catch up when father honked the horn. We began to make better time.

"This is more like it," father shouted. "We'll be home by morning if we don't freeze."

He turned to smile at me, and the car crashed gently into an obstruction and stalled again.

Out we piled and saw before us, none the worse for her encounter, a sad-faced Jersey cow.

"I know just how she feels," father cried. "Where the mischief did she come from?"

[223]

I wanted to shoo her aside and hurry on, but father refused.

"Some other fools may be on the road tonight. Either they or Bossy might be killed. She belongs in a field somewhere. Let's find it." Fifteen minutes later we stumbled on a corral, well off the road, its gates ajar. Father slapped Bossy on the flank and, with encouraging shouts, guided her to safety and closed the gate.

Warmed by the exercise, we proceeded on our way.

"How did you know," I asked, raising my voice against the ominous wind, "that the cow wouldn't kick when you slapped her?"

"Oh, it's like anything else," father replied. "You learn. Cattle are cantankerous critters. But they—*Say!*

Did you ever see a herd of cattle when its security was menaced? The cattle organize as a unit. It's an instinct. In my church everyone is fighting someone else. Suppose I appear as a threat to everybody. Wouldn't they all get together on being mad at me? Once they get together, wouldn't they build the church?"

That did not sound like a very good idea to me. "And where will that leave you?" I asked.

"Oh, don't worry about that," father replied. "We'd have to move, of course. But that's the only way we'll ever get this church built."

He stared hard at the road ahead and in a moment repeated, "Yes, that's the only way."

I knew what he was thinking, for my thoughts were the same. A pastor's future depends on his success. Churches like to have a winner for a preacher. And if, suddenly, father left Park Hill in the midst of a building program, he would be branded throughout Methodism as a man who couldn't finish his job.

My head rang with the comments ministers would make at the next Conference: "Dr. Spence? Oh, I'm afraid he's slipping. He couldn't finish the Park Hill job, you know."

"Dr. Spence? He's gone to an easier job, back in Iowa."

From the grimness of father's face I knew that these thoughts and many more were assailing him, too. Where would the bishop send him now? What church would want him?

For two hours we drove on in silence. But as we reached the paved highway and safer driving father sat back and smiled once more.

[225]

"Now, we'll get someplace," he said, pulling the throttle down to thirty miles an hour.

The next morning father telephoned the bishop and gained his consent to a campaign of alienation. He then telephoned the banker, Haynes Potter, at his office.

"Haynes, what's this scheme you tried to put over in my absence?"

"It's not a scheme at all," the banker replied hotly, resenting father's choice of words. "It's good sound business practice. I merely proposed that we finance the church in the modern manner instead of resorting to the slipshod method of cramming pledges down people's throats and then forcing them to pay. My bank would be glad to lend the church a quarter of a million dollars and take a mortgage on the property."

"You bet your sweet life you would," father retorted, "at six per cent interest."

"These days that is a very modest rate."

"Not for a church, Mr. Potter. There's only one way to finance a church, and that is to go out and raise the money first."

"Nonsense. That's old-fashioned and impractical. It is much more businesslike to retire bonds at regular intervals and spread the payments over a period long enough that no one will be pinched."

"I don't agree," father challenged him. "And anyway I think the pastor of the church should be consulted before any such proposition is submitted to the finance committee."

"I'm afraid, Doctor," Mr. Potter said, "that you are

more concerned with your prerogatives than with our financing problem."

"Well," father said, bringing the conversation to a close, "at least my prerogatives don't cost six per cent."

Within a few weeks a subtle change took place among the congregation. The spread of animosity among the various groups ceased. Men who had scarcely been on speaking terms began to put their heads together in corners. At the Wednesday suppers low-voiced conversations broke up if father passed. Committees began to meet as often as once a fortnight, but through odd circumstances the chairman usually forgot to notify father in advance.

In public father wore a worried expression. At home he played the piano with gusto and hummed little tunes. He was constantly on the lookout for new ways to irritate his members.

In February Eileen returned from a party almost in tears. Several of her friends had made uncomplimentary remarks about father. Under his coaxing she finally confessed with quivering lips, "Mary Ellen Miller says everyone in the church wants you to leave, and her father said that for half a dollar he'd lead the fight against you himself."

"Is that so?" father answered. "Well, don't you worry about it. I had no idea you children would become involved in this, but pay no attention. Just remember that it's exactly what I want."

At the next Wednesday-night supper he sought out Harvey Miller.

"I understand you'd like to have a new pastor."

"Why, what makes you say that?"

"Nothing at all," father said. "But I warn you, I'm a tough man to get rid of."

Despite the fact that nearly everyone wanted to oust father, he was also admired for apparently holding his ground against the opposition.

"Dr. Spence," they would say at dinner parties, "is a wonderful man and the best preacher we ever had. But he is so stubborn about getting his own way that we'll never get the church built while he's here."

Of course, father heard these comments. They made him more stubborn. As a result, before the winter ended the church people were beginning to agree on a set of blueprints that father had not seen.

Father went to the bishop's residence, told him that the job was done, and returned home radiant.

"Mother," he exclaimed, "if the bishop would shake my hand again as he did this morning, I'd go through it once more. But we won't have to; he's sending us to the best salary of our lives!"

On the fifth of April we moved—back again into the midwest. But not until the bishop told them at the dedication did the Park Hill congregation learn that father deliberately had turned them against him, knowing that if they could agree on ousting their pastor they would agree on church plans, too.

Later, when we returned to the mountains for a vacation, we were received enthusiastically. It became father's custom to go to Denver for his holiday year after year. Much as he loved the Iowa plains, the deep, calm quiet of the hills fascinated him as did perhaps nothing else in his life. He wrote his best sermons about the mountains and gave them appropriate names: *The Mountaintop of*

Christian Experience, Sundown at Timberline, and *Snow Trails through the Pines.*

Not even the prospect of a drive across Nebraska, where the wind burns like a blast furnace on August days, could deter him if he had any excuse to visit Colorado. And the entire family shares this enthusiasm. Friendships formed in Park Hill became enduring, and, when their schooling ended, Eileen and Fraser both settled in Denver.

22

ONE town in father's ministry must remain nameless. For convenience I shall call it Riverton, and shall not identify by actual name any of its residents. The city was notable chiefly for its insincerity and entrenched smugness. Ruling the populace were a few pioneer descendants of great wealth; with nothing to do, they made a profession of defeatism.

The town was beautiful to look upon. Built on five hills overlooking the Mississippi river, Riverton was opulent with handsome homes set in expensive lawns, with clean stores, wide streets, and many churches. But, like the river, which was sluggish because its current had been blocked by a power dam twenty miles downstream, the town had lost its drive and, dammed by economic forces that took commerce from the river to the railroads, it, too, stagnated.

Father's church was ruled by an oligarchy whose ancestors had organized the first Methodist church west of Chicago. And dominant in the ruling class was Preston Thurston, Riverton's merchant prince. He was three inches under six feet tall, but his officiousness added mightily to his stature, and he wore a vast mane of hair that increased his height and impressiveness.

Thurston was a leather manufacturer, with a large store on the main thoroughfare. He owned three blocks of business properties and was a director of two banks and of the leading department store. In the church not only did he have power of veto over every official action but he and his clique ran the choir, singing Sunday after Sunday with voices that had long since succumbed to the corrosions of age.

During his career father encountered many church bosses but never such a man as Thurston. This keystone of Riverton's business and social life was chairman of the official board, superintendent of the Sunday school, choirmaster, church treasurer, and chairman of the pastoral committee. His wife was superintendent of the junior department of Sunday school, leader of the Queen Esthers, and president of the Ladies' Aid. Over a period of years he had put in other vital church positions his three cousins and their wives. Together they composed the choir, with Thurston's sister as organist.

This family grip was tightened by cooperation with two other families: Mr. and Mrs. Merrill Hodges, who had made a fortune in southern lumber, and Mr. and Mrs. John Rhoades, poor relations of the Hodges family, who did all the menial tasks.

Dominated by this autocracy was a church membership of nearly one thousand, which, freed from dictation, would have constituted as fine a congregation as any preacher could desire. Before he had been in town a week father decided, for their sake, to rid the church of its yoke, clean out the choir loft, and place ecclesiastical management in the hands of men and women willing to work for the greater glory of God.

Such a program would terrify any preacher, but once he had made up his mind father attacked with vigor. He decided to make a deep impression on members of the parish not accustomed to receiving attention from their pastors.

His first opportunity came at the reception two weeks after we arrived. More than three hundred attended. The scene was the church basement, a large concrete-floored room used by the Sunday school and Epworth League. As he stood in the receiving line, meeting the three hundred, father scanned each face for the intelligence and courage he was going to need for the task ahead. If a man or woman appeared to suit his plans he repeated the name aloud during the introduction.

"Dr. Spence, this is Mr. Paulsen."

"Mr. *Paulsen?*" father said, giving the name heavy emphasis.

"That's right."

"And what is your first name, Mr. *Paulsen?*"

"Roger C."

"Roger C. Paulsen," father repeated. "Very happy to know you."

So it went throughout the evening. All the way home father did not speak once and was almost as silent for the three remaining days until Sunday. This was so unusual that we knew he was working at something. Sunday morning we discovered what he had been doing. After church, when he was shaking hands with the congregation, he greeted more than a hundred persons by name—not just the surname but first name and middle initial—and he did not make a single mistake.

[232]

His next job was to find out who among the hundred were Thurston retainers or sympathizers. This took all summer. He went fishing and golfing with the men, took us on all-day picnics to the river cottages of members of the congregation, and made scores of pastoral calls. By September he had organized a devoted group of eleven families eager to help him and was ready for action against the Thurstons.

But he did not assert himself until October, when the first Quarterly Conference met to perfect an organization for the winter. The presiding district superintendent was on father's side. As usual, Preston Thurston had prepared a schedule of appointments for all the important offices and board vacancies. It was the rule, by Thurston's decree, that the preacher call on Thurston, who, in turn, read out the assignments. Since father had given him no reason to suspect defiance he was wholly unprepared to hear father read a list of his own. Thurston was forced to keep silent. Father, however, had been shrewd enough not to overthrow the oligarchy from important posts. What he did was to name his friends to the official board, leaving Thurston as its chairman. He also skillfully manipulated assignments to give himself a majority on the music committee.

After the conference Thurston strode up to father.

"Dr. Spence, it is customary in this church to turn the appointments over to me. We've done it that way for years."

"Oh, I'm sorry," father replied serenely. "It will probably take me quite awhile to master all your traditions."

He smiled so disarmingly that Thurston decided he had

not been slighted deliberately and went out to make excuses to his disappointed followers.

Father's next move was to reorganize the choir. Choir singers are a peculiar breed: "a cross," as father used to say, "between the devil's grandmother and a mountain wildcat." The choir is usually composed of the exhibitionists in the parish. They like having the attention of the congregation focused on them Sunday after Sunday, and they take their solos as seriously as opera stars. If they would resign when their voices crack there might be a semblance of harmony in most churches. But choir singers refuse to surrender, even though the whole congregation laughs at their pathetic efforts.

It had been immediately apparent to father that he must maneuver with unusual caution if he was going to effect any change in his choir at Riverton. They were organized to protect their jobs and had such a tenacious rein on church politics that they were able to obstruct every constructive activity within the church.

During summer talks with laymen at their river cottages father learned that on Christmas Sunday most of the congregation remained away from service because on that day the choir took over, the pastor merely acting as presiding officer for an hour of music. Every year the choir sang the same cantata, each year a little worse. Christmas Sunday, which should be one of the most spiritual of the year, had degenerated into a field day for Preston Thurston.

Father realized that the time to put a stop to this practice was during his first year at Riverton. Otherwise he, too, would become entwined in Thurston's proudest custom. So early in the autumn he began making plans that would include a solution to another situation that worried him.

He had grieved all summer that none of the younger generation attended his services. The children went to Sunday school, then disappeared. He and mother discussed the problem for weeks. Finally mother asked permission to organize a junior service of worship. Her proposal was to use the basement rooms for a church of her own, with only the children present. She would follow the adult ritual until time for a sermon, then segregate her charges into age groups for classroom study, with high school seniors as teachers.

Father's new friends on the official board accepted the suggestion, and mother began the first Sunday in October with twenty-two children. By mid-November attendance had increased to a hundred and fifty. One of her projects was hymn singing, and along with the "Songs of Praise" she taught several Christmas anthems.

On Dec. 1 she reported to father that she was ready, whereupon he went to the shoe store of his staunchest friend, Shepherd Saunderson, whom he had appointed chairman of the music committee.

"Shep," he said, "there's to be a board meeting next week, and I think someone ought to report on the young people's progress. I want you to attend the children's service on Sunday in order to make a report."

"Gladly, Dr. Spence," Saunderson replied.

"And listen to the singing, Shep," father suggested. "Maybe it's a solution to our Christmas problem."

Saunderson nodded. "I think I'm beginning to see what you mean," he said, smiling broadly. "I certainly will do all I can."

He heard the children sing and then proposed to the official board that they be invited "upstairs" on Christmas Sunday. Since this would assure a full audience for the cantata for the first time in years, Preston Thurston did not object.

Next Saunderson suggested that the children be put in the balcony in a body. "Let's let the church see them together," he explained. "You'll be amazed at the large number of youngsters who are attending that service every Sunday."

That, too, was approved.

Delicately, then, Saunderson praised the children's wonderful singing and, as though by a sudden happy inspiration, moved that the juniors be invited to sing the Christmas music.

Thurston was on his feet immediately to exercise his power of veto. But in order to engage in the debate he had to surrender the presiding chair to the vice-chairman, Roger Paulsen. And Paulsen, accepting the gavel, immediately recognized Mr. Parsons, another of father's friends, and ignored Thurston's demand that he be heard.

"I want to second Mr. Saunderson's motion." Parsons said quickly. "I have three children in Mrs. Spence's service, and in the last few weeks our Sunday-dinner conversation has been dominated by a very exciting recital of what my girls are learning. Our children need recognition. This church has not given them any for twenty years. And we certainly cannot expect this church to live unless the children become active in it."

Thurston tried to make himself heard. "I say *no*," he shouted, "and I mean *no!* Our cantata has been a Christmas tradition for thirty-four years, and we are not going to upset it now."

But sentiment was against him. Paulsen put the issue to a vote, and the children won the day. But neither Thurston nor the Thurston Digbys nor the Preston Digbys nor the Wendell Digbys nor the Hodges nor the Rhoadeses attended the Christmas service. Even Miss Elsa Thurston developed a headache, and a substitute organist played that day.

23

FATHER tolerated the choir for another year and a half. It took that long to strengthen his position sufficiently to risk open warfare.

One morning he returned from church with a headache.

"I'm not going to preach another Sunday with that gang caterwauling behind me," he announced. "I've heard Louella Digby sing 'When a mother stills her child' for the last time."

He invited the children's service to provide music the following Sunday. After the children's anthem he made a speech.

"Nothing is so rich to a father as the sound of his children's voices," he said. "I'm sure our Heavenly Father is as pleased as we are with the fine singing we have just heard. A happy thought has occurred to me. Our loyal choir has had no rest for nearly twenty years." He looked over his shoulder at Mrs. Thurston. She was sitting in the choir loft with the regulars, all of whom were there, even though they had nothing to do. "That's right, isn't it, Sister Thurston?"

"Twenty-four years," she corrected him with a smile, though furious at this public attention to her age.

"Yes," father went on, "twenty-four years. That is service deserving of reward. Why don't you good singers take a vacation this summer? We'll let the children sing."

That was my cue. From a seat among the children in the balcony I started to applaud. The juniors added their hand clapping to mine. So, too, did half the adults.

"All right," father called, stilling the demonstration. "I accept that applause as a tribute to our faithful choir.

[239]

Over the summer we'll let you rest. The children will carry on."

Father survived many fights during his ministry, but never did he experience one so vitriolic and abusive as that which followed. The choir was outraged. Its members severally and jointly threatened to resign from the church, but father stood his ground.

"I cannot withdraw from a public announcement," he told them. "Moreover, the children would be disappointed. After all, you should be glad for a chance to rest after all these years."

But they were not glad. Thurston threatened to break Shepherd Saunderson in business unless the choir was reinstated. That failing, he told several church members in his employ that he would dismiss anyone whose children sang with the juniors. He telephoned the district superintendent and the bishop. But he could not withdraw his financial support to the church without resigning as treasurer, which he would not do.

The choir continued to come to church, but only in order to protect their jobs. However, in the autumn it was apparent that father had no intention of restoring the old organization to the loft. Instead, he proposed to the board that since the young people had done so well they should be given a chance to join the choir for the winter.

"I'll sing with no youngsters," Thurston objected. "Neither will my wife nor any of the Digbys."

"In that case," father retorted, "we acknowledge your fine spirit of cooperation and self-sacrifice and can only regret that you and your family no longer will be singing for the church."

Thurston left the meeting. In his absence a new choir was organized, with the high school music teacher as organist and director.

A month later, when the church appointments were read, Thurston was dislodged from his post as chairman of the official board. He could not complain, for he was not speaking to father.

The repercussions were immediate.

Father learned that a detective agency had been employed to trace his history as far back as college for some stigma that could be whispered about and bring him low.

"I'm not worried," he said. "My past is as clean as a hound's tooth."

A month later Eileen, now a freshman at Ohio Wesleyan university, wrote home that a strange man had been following her about the campus.

In reply father wrote: "I always knew that the choir had leather lungs, but I didn't think the echo would carry quite so far. Apparently they will stop at nothing to get me out of town. But with your Heavenly Father to guide you, you have nothing to fear."

By springtime the new choir was firmly established, and resentment seemed to be dying out. Then one day the high school principal, a member of our church, called me to his office.

"Hartzell," he said, "I scarcely know how to say what I must say."

"I don't know of anything I've done recently," I replied, "but go ahead. I suppose it was that editorial about the stupidity of teaching geometry to students interested in English."

"No," he sparred, "you've done a good job with the paper; I'm proud of it. You're the best cheer leader we've had in some time. We are counting on your flute in the orchestra concert. It's because you are so prominent in school that I'm embarrassed."

"What's the trouble?"

Mr. Haskins nervously wiped his brow and blew his nose.

"Hartzell, I've got to suspend you."

"Suspend me?" I repeated, dumbfounded.

"Yes."

"What have I done?"

"Don't you know?"

"Why—I haven't the faintest idea. That was all a mistake, throwing that Christmas decoration full of water at Miss Mitchell. I apologized."

"No, no, it's not that. Hartzell, do you know Elsie Mayfield?"

"Why, yes," I said, "She's in my Latin class."

"She's not there now."

"No," I answered. "I understand her parents moved to Chicago."

"Do you know why?"

"Why—no. I'm sure I don't know."

"You couldn't guess?"

Mystified, I asked for clarification.

"Hartzell, the Mayfields left town because their daughter is pregnant, and I'm told you're responsible."

Panicky at the mere thought of what this would do to father, I stumbled home, accepting my suspension without a word of protest. Father was in his library, writing a sermon. I entered without knocking and closed the door.

"Well, son," he greeted me, "it must be something important to bring you home at this hour."

"It is," I said sickly and told him the story.

When I finished his face was gray. He put his right fingers on his left wrist and felt his pulse, a mannerism that had grown on him with the increasing irregularity of his heartbeats.

"Son," he said earnestly, "I want you to answer me a question. If ever in your life you lied to me don't do it now. There is too much involved. If you are responsible, I'll stand behind you. If you are not responsible, someone is going to hear from me. Are you or are you not guilty?"

I stood before him and looked him in the eye. "No, sir," I replied firmly, "I'm not. I never had a date with the girl in my life."

Father sighed gently. "All right, I believe you. Have you told your mother?"

"No, sir. I came directly to you."

"Good."

He arose and seized his hat.

"I wouldn't tell your mother," he advised. "It will only worry her."

We drove back to school and confronted Mr. Haskins.

"That's a terrible story," father said. "Do you realize how it will affect me?"

Mr. Haskins looked out the window. "I'm afraid I do, Doctor."

"Where did you get it?"

"The superintendent's office called me. Mr. Partridge advised that Hartzell be suspended until it is proved or disproved."

Mr. Partridge was another member of the church.

"I'll see him," father said. "Meanwhile, I think it is unfair to suspend my son and attach that stigma to him when I believe he is telling the truth. A man is innocent until he is proven guilty. Did the Mayfield girl accuse Hartzell?"

"Not to my knowledge."

"Are you willing to take the responsibility for suspending Hartzell and perhaps ruining his life on the strength of a rumor?"

Mr. Haskins did not reply.

"Hartzell," father ordered me, "go back to class." Then, to Mr. Haskins, "I'm going down to see Mr. Partridge. I think he'll agree with me not to suspend Hartzell unless there is conclusive evidence."

For a fortnight thereafter father was unusually busy, even for him. Up and down town he drove the Ford at breakneck speed, intent on one purpose, to trace the rumor to its source.

Mr. Partridge had got the story from Mr. Moody. Mr. Moody had heard it from Mrs. Simonds. She had been told by Sister Goldthwaite. Mr. Goldthwaite had picked it up in the bank—from whom, he didn't recall.

"Then *think!*" father demanded, "or I'll go down to your bank and put every last teller through an inquisition that will put Torquemada in the shade."

Under such sternness Mr. Goldthwaite remembered. "I was told it on good authority by Mr. Claypoole."

Mr. Claypoole had overheard it at Kiwanis. He was sitting at a table with several men, and he didn't recall who had imparted the news. Off father went again to see all the men mentioned. He swept through many blind alleys and three days later emerged again on a warm

[244]

scent. The Y.M.C.A. secretary had been given the tale by the city librarian. She received it from an assistant, who had got it from one of Elsie Mayfield's friends.

"Which friend?"

"Dorothy Ledbetter."

Father smiled. Dorothy Ledbetter was the chief tale-bearer in the Kings' Daughters circle, to which Louella Digby belonged, and the Kings' Daughters were Riverton's primary gossip dispensers. Originally, when founded by Jacob Riis, the organization worked among the poor, but this objective had long been lost in Riverton.

Father went to see Dorothy Ledbetter. She had gone to tea one day at Louella Digby's and had heard the story there under her promise *never* to divulge the source. It was quite coincidental that the Kings' Daughters had met that same evening. Perhaps she had betrayed the confidence; she wasn't quite sure.

Jubilantly father went to the Digby home, sure now that he was near the goal. Mrs. Digby received him frigidly.

"I suppose," she said, "you are coming on your hands and knees now to invite us back into the choir."

"Not on your life," father replied. "I came to haul you into court and your whole tribe with you."

"Mercy me," Mrs. Digby gasped. "You'll do what?"

"Mrs. Digby," father went on firmly. "I've been waiting nearly two years for you to go too far. Now I've got you. Thank God I'm a Christian, or I'd kill you."

"Why, Dr. Spence," Mrs. Digby exclaimed, backing away, "what on earth has come over you?"

"You know," he said, with an icy smile. "You know as well as I. You thought you planted your little deception carefully. You thought it would be a fine way to get me out of town, didn't you? But you overlooked one thing, Mrs. Digby. A preacher stops being a preacher and becomes a father when his son is attacked. You tried to blacken my son to get at me. The Devil himself never thought up a more vicious scheme. I know not only what *you* did but who prompted you to do it, and I'll get every mother's son of you if it's the last act of my life."

"I don't know what you're talking about," Mrs. Digby protested feebly.

"The sure defense of the guilty," father whipped. "It's an excuse as old as the Bible. It won't do any good to add another falsehood to your sins. I've *got* you. I know the *whole* story."

Mrs. Digby sank weakly into an armchair.

"Louella Digby," father threatened, towering over her, "on Sunday I am going to tell from my pulpit what you and your crowd have done and shame you publicly."

"No!"

"Yes. You and your husband and Preston and your brothers-in-law. Every one of you."

Mrs. Digby began to cry.

"Didn't you stop to think," father asked, softening his voice, "that you can't blacken the character of a boy who has no guilt in him?"

"I —"

"You didn't even inquire whether the poor little Mayfield girl was in trouble. No, you just saw your chance to get rid of your preacher. But you see, Mrs. Digby, there's nothing the *matter* with Elsie Mayfield. Her father moved because his job took him away. And believe you me, I *know*. I went to Chicago to find out."

[246]

He let the implications entrench themselves, then continued. "You crucified a guiltless boy. You got together with the whole clan and hatched the scheme. Wendell lived across the street from the Mayfields. He saw them leave town. He brought you the news. And between you, you thought up this dirty story. Didn't you?"

She shook her head.

"Didn't you?" he insisted.

Slowly she nodded.

"And you figured out how best to spread it without getting caught, didn't you? Tell the Kings' Daughters, and they'll do the rest, you said. Didn't you!"

She covered her eyes with a handkerchief.

"Mrs. Digby, you don't deserve to live. The only reason you don't die is because the good Lord wouldn't know what to do with you."

He started toward the door.

"What are you going to do?" she asked.

Father returned and looked down at her. "I could sue you for criminal libel," he said, "but that would be unchristian. I could horsewhip your menfolk, but that wouldn't help any."

He paused, to clear the atmosphere, and set his listener for the verdict he had long since decided to impose upon the guilty.

"Mrs. Digby," he announced, "I'm going to hold a revival meeting. At the first altar call I want every last member of your family to walk up and pray forgiveness for this terrible sin you have committed. If you don't— right then and there I will make a public confession for you and *demand* that you come forward."

24

Ⓣʀᴜᴇ to his word, father held a spring revival.

But it was several weeks delayed. He was convinced that the appeal must be in keeping with the spirit of the nineteen twenties. Therefore, he postponed the session until he could formulate a new program. When this was finally perfected only the revival hymns were retained from his former campaign pattern.

Before announcing the revival he called for volunteers to take a religious census. When a sufficient number had responded he divided the city into sections and assigned them to various workers. These workers inquired at each house whether the family was affiliated with a church. The answers were carefully annotated. The names of families that had drifted from the Catholic church, or whose members expressed such a preference, were turned over to the priest at St. John's. The information pertaining to Jewish families was sent to Rabbi Haman at the synagogue. The remainder were re-sorted in groups of ten and temporarily put aside.

Father then announced that a revival would start the next Sunday and run for three weeks. Following this, he sent personal notes to Preston Thurston, the Digby families, and their connections to remind them of their special obligation.

The revival started as any ordinary Sunday-morning service would have. The prelude was played, the Call to Worship was sung, and the Order of Worship was followed until the sermon began. The sermon was a message of repentance, preceded by a candid statement that traditional exhortations were outmoded and therefore would not be indulged in and followed by an altar call.

As the call went forth, father's glance singled out Preston Thurston and his wife, the Thurston Digbys, the Wendell Digbys, and the Rhoadeses. Their hour had come. A tingle of excitement electrified the congregation.

"If any man or woman," father intoned, "this day desires to confess a particular sin and before God and this company of witnesses sincerely plead forgiveness, let him come forward now."

Mercifully the organ intruded on the silence. Father looked at Preston Thurston and waited. The organ finished one verse of a hymn and began another. Still father waited, unmoving and unmoved. The hymn had almost ended when Preston Thurston arose. He looked across the aisle at the rest of the clan. They likewise arose. Thurston nodded and, leading the way, walked slowly to the altar rail and knelt.

"God bless you," father said and knelt beside them.

That evening nearly two hundred church members, including Preston Thurston, remained in their pews after the service. Father had asked them to stay, following the benediction.

"The time has passed," he explained, "for the old-fashioned revival to accomplish God's work on earth. The appeal must meet conditions as they exist today. Here's what we are going to do."

He divided the penitents into teams of five each. To each team he gave ten cards that had disclosed, in the census, a Protestant family without church affiliation.

"Instead of bringing the sinners to the revival," father said, "we are going to take the revival to them. On each card there is a name. I want you to go in twos and threes to each of these homes. Make an appointment in advance. Tell them you wish to talk to them about God's business. Make it a business call. Try to sell them the idea that they are missing the greatest thing in life in not professing and living Christianity. Try to get them out next Sunday to our church service. If they come sit with them, and when the altar call is voiced you will know what to do."

During the ensuing three weeks every home was visited, and, of more than 1,600 persons approached, 900 responded. Of these 176 joined father's church. The others united with suburban Methodist charges or other denominations.

Father's greatest triumph was not the number reached, however, but one particular interview that did not even end in a conversion.

For years Dr. Harlan Horrigan, an unusually skilled dentist, had been the town's outspoken skeptic. He prided himself in laughing at all religion, particularly Christianity. Wherever there was a revival meeting he would surely appear, not to worship but to scoff.

"It's better entertainment than the Kiwanis minstrels," he said.

Father's personal-visitation campaign intrigued Dr. Horrigan. Here was a new technique. He attended the first two Sunday services, sitting in the balcony. Several times during the week he entered the church to watch the "little meetings," during which the solicitors dropped in to report their progress and fortify their faith for renewed effort.

Father watched him. Twice Dr. Horrigan deliberately crossed his path at the church door, trying to provoke him, but father merely smiled.

The third week father acted. He sauntered into the dentist's office just at noon, when the receptionist was at lunch.

"It would appear," he remarked dryly, looking around the empty office, "that I have a larger practice than you have."

"Come in, come in," Dr. Horrigan invited. "I'm delighted to see you. I wondered when you'd get round to me."

"Oh, I'm not here professionally," father answered. "I was in Dr. Updegraf's office, and I saw you here alone. I just want to ask you a question."

"Shoot," Dr. Horrigan said suspiciously.

"Well, it's this. You have been watching revivals with an impartial eye for a good many years, I'm told."

"That's right. Best show on earth. Better than a circus. When people make monkeys of themselves, it's amusing."

"Indeed it is," father agreed. "As an expert skeptic and one not likely to be swayed emotionally, what do you think of my new method?"

"What do you mean?"

"Well, you and I both will agree, probably, that the

old-time revival is through. People don't respond to it any more."

"That's right."

"Do you think personal visitation is any better?"

"Well—"

"Come, come," father coaxed. "I'm not trying to convert you. I'm serious about this. It's my job. I have to find a way to get under the hides of people in a very materialistic world. Am I on the right track?"

"I wouldn't be surprised. At least you are appealing to reason, not to the emotions. My chief argument against religion is that it is an emotional appeal. There's no intelligence in it."

"Perhaps you're right," father continued. "Christianity has been sold the wrong way. It's like getting a drunkard to sign the pledge without curing his thirst."

"Exactly."

"That's why I'm trying to sell Christianity on a business basis. My competitor is indifference or skepticism. I have to make the Christian way of life better in every way than skepticism, or it won't stay sold. Just as I'd be sure, if I were a shoe salesman, that my product was better than that of any of my competitors."

"I see your point," Dr. Horrigan admitted, "but I still don't think you have anything to sell."

"Why not?"

"Because basically you are peddling something there's no truth in. How do we know Christ was the Son of God? He was a teacher whose philosophy had a great impact on civilization. But so was Karl Marx. So was Confucius. Are they any less divine? The philosophy of Confucius was merely a practical code. Sensible men would think and act the same way if they had never heard of Confucius. Jesus came into a chaotic world and restored it to order merely by being practical. If anything, He was an opportunist. That doesn't prove He was divine or that there is any divinity. Science will catch up with you clerics one of these days and prove you wrong. Then what?"

"Then the world will be much the poorer," father answered. "Even if Christ were not divine, His teaching has survived, where the teaching of the Romans, the Greeks, the Egyptians, the Chinese, all have been rejected by the Western world. Christ's teaching was the one single force that released men from the dark age of ignorance and made possible this modern world. Without Christianity, there would be no enlightenment as we know it."

"Perhaps that's true," Dr. Horrigan conceded. "I'll admit the Christian philosophy made Western civilization possible. But I still say it was and is *only* a philosophy."

"Then you will admit that as a philosophy, if not as a religion, it is worth while?"

"As a philosophy, yes. As a religion, no."

"And you will concede that without this philosophy we would have no modern world at all?"

"Somebody else would have expressed the same ideas, because we needed them."

"All right, but the man who *did* express them was *Jesus*, and you ought to respect Him for it."

"As a philosopher, I do."

"Do you laugh at Confucius?"

"No."

"Then why do you laugh at Jesus?"

"I don't laugh at Jesus, I laugh at Christianity."

"Well," father chuckled, "at times it does seem funny, I'll admit. But it is the best thing we have. And it would be a lot better if these poor instruments God has to work with had more backbone. I feel better now that I know you are not making fun of Christ."

"I'm just laughing at all religion, that's all."

"I'm glad to know that," father said. "But why can't you leave the religious angle out of Christianity, and respect it merely as a good rule for living? You live the Christian life yourself, you just don't profess it."

"Well, I suppose maybe that's so."

"All right, then. When you laugh at Christianity you laugh at the very rules you live by. Do you laugh at Clyde Potter because he still drives a horse when everyone else is riding in automobiles?"

"No, of course not."

"You respect his belief in the infallibility of the horse?"

"Of course."

"Then all I ask of you," father concluded, "is that you respect our belief in Christianity as a religion. You don't have to believe it, but you are just professing narrowness when you laugh at it. You respect Christ as a teacher, I'll respect Him as the Son of God, and we'll both be happy."

Father was surprised, on the closing Sunday of the revival, to see Dr. Horrigan again in the audience. He had pondered long over their conversation and had built his final sermon not as a defense of Christianity but as a great rule of conduct that all men should respect for what it had accomplished, whether or not they were Christians.

"But we, as Christians," he said, "are happier than those who practice Christianity without believing in it. For we have the courage of conviction. We have God the Father and Christ His Son to turn to when we need encouragement. When a man's wife dies a rule of conduct is little comfort. The hope of eternity is great and consoling, but it must be believed. There are some things a man accepts on faith. The dentist does not have to be told, when he sees severe erosion in a tooth, that there is a cavity beneath. He knows and, seeking, he finds it. We Christians do not have to be told there is an eternal life. We know. And, seeking, we find it."

He looked directly at Dr. Horrigan then and quoted a verse of Scripture: "If any man will do the will of my Father in Heaven, he shall know whether the doctrine be of God or whether I speak it of myself."

Once again he offered the altar call. And this time Dr. Horrigan did not laugh.

25

~

RIVERTON was a city of brilliant weddings, and father greatly enjoyed a big church ceremony. Most of the couples he married were not members of his parish, however, but rural residents who came to town for their license and then rushed to the nearest minister.

As time went on he developed a matrimonial formula to brighten the ceremony and bring happiness to the bride. He knew that a pair who could afford to give him only two dollars for his services would respond to different tactics from those he used most successfully with a bridal party that expected to pay five dollars. He had learned to gauge quickly the financial status of the bridegroom and had developed a set of jokes for each price range.

Father believed that, except for the solemn three-minute religious ritual, a wedding should be a joyous occasion. He was annoyed if the bride's mother wept or the bride was tight-lipped and nervous. In parsonage ceremonies he kept up a running fire of wit while he filled in the official license. This served to put the bridal party at ease and also contrasted with his solemnity during the actual ritual.

His two-dollar patter began like this: "Be careful how you answer these questions, young lady. It's perjury to falsify your age on a marriage record."

His five-dollar opening was: "Come in, come in. So you want to be married. Well, young man, I don't blame you. You're wise to get a ring on this young lady's finger before someone else does." Then, turning to the bride: "I'll bet it took some tall talking to get *you* on the dotted line."

When he reached the question of the bride's age, his two-dollar form was: "Age next birthday?" And, receiving the answer: "You're too young to be married. Wait a year, and somebody better may turn up." He would disarm the bridegroom with a smile.

But for five dollars the bride got this: "This next question is about your age. I'll put it down as 'legal' to save your telling a fib on your wedding day." That made a hit, particularly with the middle-aged.

After the ceremony father would say, for two dollars: "All right, kiss her now. That's what you've been waiting for."

For five dollars: "All right, you're married, and if you don't hurry up and kiss the bride, young man, I'll do it myself."

Father always gave the bride a little souvenir, a book in which she could enter mementos of her wedding day. On presenting this album, father's two-dollar explanation was: "Here's a little remembrance of your wedding. There's a page in the back to list your children when the time comes." But with the five-dollar souvenir he offered:

"Get your husband to write a very endearing message on the first blank page. If he ever gets ornery you can get it out and show it to him."

After the ceremony father's first act was to return to his study and record the event in a large ledger. He set down the names and addresses of the principals, a description and the cost of his present to the bride, the cost of pressing his clothes, if such was involved, and finally the fee he received. In 1919 he began to add another entry: whether he or mother pocketed the fee, for in that year they began dividing such perquisites. During his ministry father performed 1,677 weddings.

In one town we lived opposite the county jail. The sheriff brought father the "shotgun" weddings. Invariably the sheriff wore his side arms until father asked him to remove them during the religious ceremony, and invariably the sheriff provided the wedding ring. Father hated this task. But he reasoned that if the couple had been licensed by the county his obligation was ended; and if the law demanded that a pair of youngsters marry he must obey the law.

By the time he reached Riverton father had developed a technique for large church weddings, too. But, strangely enough, the largest wedding at which he ever officiated was one of his most unpleasant experiences. The bride I will call Sarah Sanborn.

The Sanborns were of Riverton's society folk. They upheld its traditions of selfishness and narrowness, and attended church haphazardly. Only when one of them died or was married or when they needed the church building in which to celebrate a family milestone did

they consult their pastor. But on such rare occasions they greatly taxed his strength.

Sarah was twenty, high-strung and beautiful in a brittle way. She had been educated at Miss Wilks's Country Day school, followed by two years of "finishing" at Stevens college. Her bridegroom was Robert McBride Ingersoll, of the patent-medicine Ingersolls, a graduate of Harvard Law school and Riverton's only three-goal polo player.

To witness this merger of two aristocratic families, Sarah invited 1,200 guests to the church. The reception, however, was to be more exclusive.

Father explained all the rites and proprieties to Sarah and her mother one afternoon at the parsonage. Mrs. Sanborn was so bewildered that she consulted a social secretary, who, of course, upset everything. Three telephone conversations failed to settle the problem, so father was compelled to forego his customary Saturday-afternoon quiet and spend two hours at the Sanborn house. This, of course, affected his Sunday sermons, and he felt that churchgoers as intermittent as the Sanborns had no right to make such demands on him.

Thus he was not feeling very cooperative at the rehearsal the following Monday. The bride and groom, the five bridesmaids and their attending ushers, and the bride's parents came boisterously to the church from a cocktail party. Father met them at the altar. He had already arranged with the sexton for white carpeting down the bride's aisle and engaged the church organist for music. Now he must put the wedding party through the long ritual. He was weary from two Sunday services. The levity of the bridal party within the church annoyed him, and he was outraged that they had entered a house of worship stimulated by alcohol.

Patiently, nevertheless, he explained the proprieties of church weddings, pointed out the formalities step by step, and showed everyone exactly what to do.

"All right now," he concluded, "let's run through it."

The bride, of course, had a proxy. Sarah sat in a front pew. After many long delays the bridesmaids reached their stations. The arrangement pleased father. But Sarah objected.

"Darling," she called to her sister, "if you will stand a little more sidewise your dress will show off *much* better."

Father, who had strained to hold his temper before the inebriated group, now lost his patience. "Young woman," he said, "this is a religious ceremony, not a fashion show. It is shameful enough of you to come into the Lord's temple with liquor on your breaths, without turning the wedding into a parade of mannequins." The bridal party sobered immediately.

The rehearsal lasted until midnight, and father returned home exhausted. But the next night, during the wedding, he was at his best.

He arrived well ahead of the hour in order to check every detail. He met the bridegroom and best man and gave them a last-minute pep talk. Then he hurried to the vestibule and whispered a little joke to the bride so that she would come down the aisle smiling.

Once the music started, father, a master of the lock step, opened the door of his study and stepped into the pulpit. By the longest possible route he walked to the altar, timing his movements so that the bridegroom and

best man, who followed him, reached the altar just ahead
of the first bridesmaid.

Calmly he turned and winked at the bride, who by
that time was starting down the aisle on the arm of her
nervous, tearful father. The bride smiled, and father
beamed in answer. Sarah reached the altar radiant.

From that moment father was all dignity. He waited
patiently while the bride handed her bouquet to her
sister, then intoned with the full resonance of his voice:
"Dearly beloved, we are gathered here in the sight of
God, and in the presence of these witnesses, to join this
man and this woman in Holy matrimony. The family is
the foundation of human fellowship. And marriage is
not to be entered into by any inadvisedly, but reverently,
discreetly, and in the love of God."

Here he looked helpfully at the bridegroom, who too
conspicuously looked as though he wanted a strong drink.
If father had known that Robert McBride Ingersoll
already had fortified himself from a bottle of bootleg
liquor there would have been no ceremony. The bride
knew. She could smell Sen Sen on his breath, and wished
she had thought of that artifice herself.

Father couched the ceremony in the language he
reserved for great occasions. Every word of the ritual
could be heard distinctly in the last packed row of the
balcony, yet he did not raise his voice. He was dressed in
his best: cutaway coat without a wrinkle in it, trousers
razor-edged, shoes shined. His ascot tie, his wing collar,
his gray double-breasted vest all were correct. The Sanborn wedding had cost him forty dollars, including his
present to the bride and the souvenir book, but he expected to be reimbursed. Had Sarah Sanborn been a

graduate of his Sunday school and a regular worshiper he would not have accepted a wedding fee. But Ingersoll was an outsider and Sarah practically so.

After the ceremony, he waited ten minutes in his study, but the best man did not come near him. For his perfect ceremony he received not even gracious thanks. And as he waited he suddenly realized that he and his family had not been invited to the reception.

Indignant, smarting under the actual expense, which, with a daughter of his own in college, he could ill afford, he walked slowly home. Mother met him with praise.

"It was the best wedding service you ever conducted. It was beautiful."

"You think so, really?"

"Yes," said mother, whose turn it was to receive the wedding fee. "How much did you get for it?"

"Not a sou," father answered, "not a sou. But then, that's typical of Riverton."

Down the street floated the strains of an orchestra on the Sanborn lawn. Above everything in the world father loved a wedding reception.

For a moment he was entranced by the music. Then he walked indignantly upstairs to his desk, addressed an envelope to Robert McBride Ingersoll, and rolled a sheet of paper into his typewriter. Leaning over the machine, he deliberated for some time. Then, with a smile, he typed the following:

For professional services rendered: $100.00

26

❦

THE social life of Riverton was divided geographically.
On North Hill and the river-bluff sections of South Hill
lived the aristocrats. Other social groups had their
colonies, too. The little shopkeepers owned their bunga-
lows in Sunnyside; the salesmen, mechanics, and artisans
inhabited West Hill. The rest of the town was dominated
by factories and their employees. So powerful was the
caste system that children from one hill did not go to
parties on another. The result was that, through the
years, cliques had developed that, by the time of our
arrival, had become almost hereditary.

The parsonage was on North Hill, and we children
should have drawn our playmates from among our
neighbors, but anyone not born on North Hill had little
chance of acceptance. I finally broke through because
we had a Model T Ford. No one else in the group owned
an automobile disreputable enough to carry an ice-cream
freezer to picnics without ruining the car. Consequently,
the group either invited me or went without ice cream.
Fraser was accepted because the girls in his age group
outnumbered the boys two to one, and Fraser was handsome. The superficial justification for approving Fraser
and me was that, since the church had been standing

for a hundred years and father was its pastor, we could be accepted as boys with a hundred-year North Hill background.

Such deviousness, however, could not be stretched to include Eileen. She was shut out simply because she did not dance. The little cliques held dancing parties every Friday night all winter long, and we children were still not allowed this pleasure.

Eileen decided that we must find some way around father's objection, and I agreed heartily. Our opportunity came through father's own activities.

The Masonic Order annually showed its collective Christian faith by attending a church service in a body. The Protestant denominations vied with each other for these visits, for the prestige and for the hundred-dollar contribution the Masons put in the collection plate. The best pews were roped off in reserve while the Knights Templar paraded to the church in plumed hats. Because father was a Thirty-second-degree Mason, the Order selected our church the first year we were in Riverton.

The Masons appeared at the doors promptly at 10:55 and filed into their reserved seats. Their families and our own members packed the rest of the church. Miss Preston played her best prelude. The choir entered. A gasp then rose and spread throughout the church. Into the pulpit father walked, proudly dressed in his own Knights Templar uniform, the cockaded hat held over his heart. The Masons were delighted. No pastor previously had carried his recognition of Masonry that far. As a result, they returned almost every year father remained in town.

The day after the service a high school football star,

whom I knew by reputation only, came over to my locker.

"I was at your church yesterday," he said. "Your father is a thirty-second-degree man."

"Yes," I replied.

"How would you like to join the De Molay?"

This junior order of Masonry, named for the French martyr Jacques De Molay, had all the social privileges of the Masonic Temple.

"I'll ask father," I promised.

That night I told Eileen of the bid, and she was enthusiastic.

"The De Molays have a dance twice a month," she pointed out. "If you were a member we could go."

"Yes," I said hesitantly, wondering if father would let me join if he knew.

I ignored the social aspects in stating the case to father. He approved.

"Join, of course," he said. "I shall be a very proud father when you take your first Masonic degree, and De Molay is a fine preparatory school."

My application for admission was accepted. Jubilantly I told Eileen. "Now," I said, "all you have to do is to get a date for the next dance."

But she had a better idea. "why don't *you* take me?" she asked.

I did, and she was so popular that I had only two dances with her.

The next day father descended upon us in the library.

"What's this I hear about you children attending a dance last night?"

"Yes, we did." Eileen spoke up quickly. "Hartzell's a

darling. He took his own sister to his first De Molay dance."

"H-m-m-m," father answered. "Do they hold these dances often?"

"Twice a month," I informed him.

He knew the time had come to surrender to the inevitable.

"You really put that over on your old dad, didn't you?" he said and looked at us rather proudly.

He did not again object to our dancing, so long as we did not patronize public dance halls.

"It's better," he said to Fraser once, "than pawing some girl in a parked car."

Riverton was a city of entrenched capital, more sensitive than most inland towns to the rise and fall of the stock market. In good years society revolved around the country club, and everyone bought a new Buick. In lean times it centered in the American Legion municipal golf course, where the upper-crust golfed alongside day laborers.

These were the later years of the Great Boom. Prosperity had seeped even to the little shopkeepers, and they aped the older families. Card playing for money prevailed. Cigar stores took bets on horse races, sold Irish sweepstakes tickets, and operated baseball and football pools. Father was wise enough not to storm from the pulpit against this materialism, particularly after his barber made $20,000 in "the market." Instead he preached sermons designed to turn as much as possible of the circulating currency into what he called "useful pursuits." Week after week he pointed out the church's need for money: for missions at home and abroad; for the poor and underprivileged, and for general funds, both local and national.

When mother suggested that perhaps he was driving a little too hard, he replied: "I don't think so. Everybody's talking about money these days, so why shouldn't I? We don't mention money enough in our churches. In the four Gospels one verse in every six relates to material possessions. In these later days the question of money has not been given the place of importance it is intended to have. God insists that the church pay its way, and the money can come only from its sympathizers. They have the money, and it's my job to get some of it away from them. You don't want me to fall down on my job, do you?"

Father had a personal reason to be conscious of money, for while everyone else was spending freely he was continually harassed by financial worries. His salary now was $4,800 a year, which, on the surface, looks handsome enough for any man. But father's was no ordinary salary. His subscription to church support was more than a tithe: $500. He gave $100 each to foreign and home missions. Arbitrarily the Conference took ten per cent of his income for an old preachers' retirement fund. Because of his position he was also clipped for every conceivable general purpose: $100 to the Community Chest, $25 to the Y.M.C.A., and a like sum to the Y.W.C.A.; $25 to the Day Nursery; $25 to the Salvation Army; and $25 to the church poor fund. In addition, $5 and $10 bills were continually leaving the parsonage for other organized charities.

To at least $2,000 spent in this way he added many

benevolences of his own. He never turned away a stranger with a hard-luck story. Some of my earliest memories are of unkempt men and women, wheedling funds from father.

I remember clearly how one day he told us he could not afford tickets to the automobile show. An hour later we saw him give seven dollars to a tramp who pretended to be a prodigal son. Next he paid the railway fare of a young man whose mother was dying in a distant city, only to learn later that the youth actually was fleeing from a robbery. Once he permitted a grafter to run up a large long-distance bill on our telephone, and a week later the call was traced by Federal officers investigating the Drake estate, a notorious Midwestern swindle. He gave transportation to a man who said his sister would be embarrassed if he returned home in an undignified manner. Of the scores of persons to whom he loaned many hundreds of dollars, only two ever repaid him: a Korean cook en route to a new job, and a Methodist minister's son who had been the victim of a pickpocket.

Both Eileen and I were in college now, and father no longer could stand this drain on his resources. One day he had to borrow money on his insurance. When he returned from downtown he brought with him a sheet of white cardboard and a ten-cent-store picture frame. He constructed a poster, at the top of which he printed in bold letters:

LIARS I HAVE KNOWN

Underneath he wrote the names of all his debtors and hung the placard conspicuously behind his desk. As he himself said, "It did the business."

The changing world by now noticeably had affected father. One day in the autumn he went duck hunting with Shepherd Saunderson, the shoe merchant. He was too impatient to be a good huntsman and, after watching Saunderson blow fruitlessly for many minutes on an artificial duck call, he turned to his friend.

"Shep," he said, "I'm not a betting character, but if I were—mind you, I said, *if* I were—I'd bet you a dollar I can do a better job on that noisemaker than you can. Give it to me. If I don't flush up a duck in five minutes I'll give you a dollar."

For nearly ten minutes he blew, probably frightening every mallard out of the county. Then, panting for breath, he reached in his pocket, took out a one-dollar bill, wrapped it around the duck caller, and returned it to Saunderson.

The day was not gameless, however, for they returned to town with three ducks each. Driving up Jefferson street, they passed the tailor shop of a parishioner, Fred Swartz, who advertised his business with a large sign that read: "We Clean Everything but Fish."

"Wait a minute, Shep," father said, and, with a broad grin, he took his ducks into the shop and put them on the counter.

The joke was on him, however, for two hours later the ducks, thoroughly cleaned, were delivered to the house: with a bill for three dollars.

Father also began to attend the performances of traveling road shows that played one-night stands at the Opera House. He was so much excited over a matinee of *The Student Prince* that he returned that evening with all of us

[270]

and our next-door neighbors. He consented one year to be an end man in the Kiwanis minstrel show. His fellow members were perturbed at first that he might object to joining the chorus in syncopated jazz tunes. After the first rehearsal the director approached him.

"Well, Doc," he asked, "are you having any trouble with those songs?"

"Why should I?" father replied. "Every one of them is stolen from an old gospel hymn."

His theater attendance became so habitual that he was deeply disappointed one day to read in the paper that a touring company would play *Abie's Irish Rose* on the night of prayer meeting. He asked mother if she thought he could postpone the midweek service from Wednesday to Thursday, but she advised against it.

Several times on the day of the play he tried to find a legitimate excuse to be absent. Finally, fifteen minutes before the church bell was to summon the worshippers, he telephoned Clark Casey, who, with a testimonial, always went to every meeting.

"Clark," father said ingratiatingly, "why don't *you* run the prayer meeting tonight? You can do it as well as I."

Casey consented, and father happily rounded up the family for an evening in the second balcony.

During our fourth year in Riverton, while father's ministry was wholly serene, Preston Thurston decided the time had come to reassert his old power.

At first father did not recognize the attack, so cunningly was it executed. Thurston had not defied father for more than two years. But he had not ceased to dream over past glories or plan to revive them. One night, while Thurston was reading in his walnut-paneled study, three men from Asbury college called. They wanted money. Secular schools always need money, and, since Asbury was in our district, our laymen were responsible for its existence. Thurston had been generous in the past. He had built Asbury's chemistry hall in honor of his father, a member of its first graduating class, and annually gave the college $5,000.

Now the college library had burned, and most of its books were destroyed. A quarter of a million dollars was needed for new volumes and a place to house them. Thurston was asked for $25,000 to start the campaign.

During the conversation Thurston learned that President Daniel was retiring. His successor must be a Methodist preacher. Thurston immediately thought of father. He promised that, should his pastor, Dr. Spence, whom he said he greatly admired, succeed Doctor Daniel, his gift would be $100,000.

The excited delegation placed this offer before the district superintendent, who telegraphed the bishop. The next day father was invited to Asbury as its president.

Such invitations were not new. Twice previously he had declined educational posts.

"My job," he explained, "is in the parish. I can hold my own with sinners, but I'm not so sure about professors."

But this time he had to be careful. Methodist preachers still followed their bishop's orders, and pastors had been moved for a consideration far less than $100,000. An additional reason for delicacy in sidestepping the offer was the fact that, following a refusal, he might be asked to "take his turn on the district."

District superintendencies are assigned to preachers with proved executive ability, and are difficult. The superintendent is never at home. Never at ease. He must visit each church under his jurisdiction four times yearly, usually preaching a sermon on each occasion. When, finally, he has "served his time," he must be a master politician to be restored to as good a church as that which he left four years before. Preachers often had mentioned father's reluctance to shoulder this burden. If he declined the presidency of Asbury and made the bishop angry he might be transferred to the district.

So he moved cautiously. But while he was still balancing on a political tightrope, Preston Thurston jumped the gun and called one evening to congratulate him on his college presidency. Immediately father saw the game and knew how to combat it. His friends went to Omaha and proved that Thurston's motive was not generosity but eagerness to have father out of Riverton so that he might again "boss" the church. Father remained in Riverton.

But now he had to be constantly on his guard, and worry over the situation began to drain his cardiac reserve. After an anxious three months mother decided for father that Thurston's continuous machinations were killing him, and that to prolong his life we must move.

Father worked out an exchange of pulpits with a pastor in North Iowa, where his ministry had begun. He spent the summer of 1929 entrenching his followers in their church positions and warned his prospective successor against giving Thurston his head. But even before our departure Thurston had begun to rise again, and sadly father set his face as he headed out of town in the

Ford, mother beside him, Fraser crowded by a trunk in the rear seat.

Up a winding hill he drove, northward toward the beloved plains that to him were home. Atop the hill was a handsome view that father always stopped to admire. Below stretched the town and the Mississippi river, sweeping toward the south.

But today father did not pause. He pressed the accelerator to the floor, leaping the Ford ahead. With eyes riveted on the road to the north, he remarked grimly to mother: "Don't look back, Hope. You might turn to a pillar of salt!"

27

❧

FATHER began to get excited long before the car reached Mason City, our new home. As soon as the country leveled off into the flat plains he became jubilant. From Charles City on, the last thirty miles of the trip were a gay homecoming.

"There's the Marsh farm," he exclaimed. "Many's the time I've eaten there."

A little later, "Now around this next bend there's as pretty a sight as you'll ever see: the cornfields are visible for ten miles."

When, finally, the shafts of the cement and tile factories of Mason City cut the horizon father increased his speed to fifty miles an hour.

"Let's go right on over to Clear Lake. I want Fraser to see this country."

Without stopping, father drove down Main Street and headed out of town.

"I know this road like a book," he shouted gleefully. "I know every tree on every farm. I've ridden it on horseback and in rigs. They straightened it out a little when they put down the paving, that's all."

[275]

He began to hum to himself.

"Those three apple trees were here thirty years ago."

Soon, "That black barn is on the Huston farm. I'd know it anywhere."

His eyes scarcely watched the road. "Now around the next corner we ought to be able to see the lake. Let's have dinner at Silsby's. Ah, *there's* a restaurant! In 1910 they served me carpet tacks in my blueberry pie. When I called Charlie Silsby's attention to them he just said, 'You preachers ask us to swallow everything you dish up; you go ahead and eat them tacks.'"

He laughed in anticipation as he pulled the Ford around the curve. But there was no lake.

"What the mischief?" he exclaimed. "Must be a little farther on."

Around many curves he drove, but the lake did not appear.

"That's funny," he grunted, "I'd have sworn we were right on it."

He explored several side roads, seeking his bearings, and eventually reached a town.

"Hampton!" father gasped. "That just goes to show how tricky your memory can be. Hampton is *south* of Mason City. Clear Lake is due *west*."

With a sheepish laugh he turned about and without another word drove to Mason City and into the driveway of the Methodist parsonage. Mother and Fraser did not see Clear Lake until the following day.

Mason City was an ideal church in an ideal town. The congregation was not wealthy; neither was it poor. It was composed of merchants and professional men and their growing families and a few farmers. The lake lured the people on Sundays, but after competing against the Rocky mountains father was unconcerned. The town was neither worldly nor naïve. It was friendly and agreeable, except for the soot from factory chimneys and dust from a cement plant.

Our house was comfortable, but, as usual with parsonages, abominably located. None of the prominent laymen would have let their families live where we made our home. On the corner was the church, a fine stone building. The parsonage was crowded against it, with a nurses' home on the other side and a hospital beyond. Across the street were the courthouse and county jail. Interurban cars to Clear Lake screeched around our corner day and night. Crowds attending a theater opposite the hospital slammed their car doors before our drive. We lived in bedlam, day and night. But the house itself was clean and livable, and in it father tried to forget the trolley cars, the traffic noises, the whining ambulance sirens, the ribaldry of prisoners. He established his study at the back of the house underneath his bedroom. Eileen was teaching school in Denver, and I was a university senior. Fraser alone of us children was at home, a high school junior.

With typical vigor father reconnoitered and found his situation ideal: the church had no debt, needed no construction, employed an efficient financial secretary for routine work and some parish calling. The membership was after father's heart: the friendly people of the Iowa plains.

Everyone in the church was working hard; there was no "boss" to conquer, and there was no discordant music. But the economic depression was a tribulation to everyone, and father was deeply pained to watch his beloved prairie folk become warped and twisted under the relentless impact of adversity. Each tragedy in the congregation was a personal blow to him. His supreme conviction was that a preacher is a failure unless his people can say of him, "Surely he hath shared our sorrows and borne our griefs."

Mother always considered father's pastoral activity his greatest attribute, although no one but her appraised correctly its magnitude, particularly at Mason City. His contact with each individual was so personal and intimate that none he helped ever realized that father likewise was comforting hundreds of others.

The people of Mason City loved him for what he meant to each of them privately, and they followed him because they loved him.

One afternoon a woman came to the parsonage in a state of intense emotional excitement.

"Dr. Spence," she moaned, "I don't know what's the matter with my husband lately. He scarcely talks to me any more, and he avoids me. I can't imagine what I've done, but I've just about decided to leave Everett if it will make him any happier."

Father asked if she had tried to find the cause of his strange behavior.

"Oh, yes," she explained, "but he won't come near me. He has always been so affectionate, but if I go to him he becomes terribly upset and leaves the house. I'd do anything in the world to help, but this morning at breakfast when I asked what was the matter he said, 'I haven't the courage to tell you,' and left the house without finishing his coffee."

Father minimized her fears and advised her to wait patiently until her husband came to her. Soon he had her laughing, and she even waved a smile to him as she climbed into her car.

About five o'clock that evening the husband rang the parsonage bell. He was one of the town's most prominent merchants, a country boy who, through enormous labor, had built a handsome business. He told father he was in trouble.

"It's about Martha. All her life she's had everything she wanted. I've worshiped the ground she walks on, and I want her to have everything. But I'm stuck. Either I put every dime I have into the business and live on practically nothing for awhile, or I'm bankrupt. I just haven't the heart to tell Martha we're broke."

"I rather imagine," father suggested, "that Martha will be as happy to share poverty with you as she was to enjoy your prosperity."

"But I haven't the heart to ask her to," Everett replied. "I was about to tell her at breakfast this morning, but she looked so doggone sweet I couldn't even talk."

Father finally gained Everett's promise that he would tell Martha the truth that night. But about three in the morning the telephone rang. Martha told him her husband had left the house before dinner and had not returned.

"What happened?" father asked.

"Nothing at all," Martha said. "I asked him if he would pay up our country-club arrears so I could give a party out there on Friday. He wrote me out a check and left the house."

Father found Everett at his Clear Lake cottage and

walked beside the water with him until after dawn. They drove home then in Everett's car, and father remained outside while Everett went in to his wife. Half an hour later Everett appeared at an upstairs window. He held up both his hands and shook them. Father went home to breakfast, then took the interurban train back to Clear Lake to pick up his Ford.

Many of his parish problems concerned youth, for there was much unemployment, and high school and college students were distraught about the future.

During an Easter holiday a young woman whose picture had often been in the papers as honors were bestowed on her at college came to him.

"Dr. Spence," she said in perplexity, "I know you are going to think I'm terrible, but I don't know what to believe any more. You know how hard mother and daddy worked to put me through school. Now it's my turn to help them. Dad's lost his job, and I can't get one, for all my training. I've worked and prayed, but neither does any good. I've always been taught to believe in the infallibility of God and capitalism, but both have let me down."

"Have they?" father asked. "Or have you let them down?"

"Why, what do you mean?" she inquired indignantly.

"I don't know," father said, "what I mean. I was merely asking a question. There is still a world, and there are still people in it. That means there is work to do. You are a dietician, aren't you?"

"Yes."

"I read in the paper the other day that at least two

million people are starving. Seems to me there's a place for a dietician there somewhere."

"But I've looked all over and can't find anything."

"I thought I heard that you were offered a job in Chicago."

"At twenty-five dollars a week! I'm not going to work for that!"

"Oh," father said. "Then there *is* work to be done. You just won't do it. Bill Hendricks is a Phi Beta Kappa from Iowa, and he's working in Smith and Henry's stationery store for twelve dollars a week. He has a baby, too. I know two lawyers who haven't seen twenty-five dollars a week since you were in high school. Jennie Carl is a waitress at the Y.W.C.A. for room and board. She was a sorority sister of yours, wasn't she?"

"Yes."

"It seems to me," father went on, "that you were offered an unusually good job for a girl just out of school. At least you have a chance to do what you were trained to do. You aren't a doctor digging ditches or an electrician running a filling station or a nurse selling millinery. I'm afraid college wasn't very good for you, Mary Ellen. If you had never gone beyond high school you wouldn't have such big ideas."

Six weeks later, at graduation time, the newspapers printed Mary Ellen's picture again, with the announcement that she had accepted a job in Chicago "with unusual opportunities."

Many situations were not so easily resolved. One case in particular upset father for months. A young man of exceptional promise was forced to stop going to college because of the death of his father. He returned home to support his three little sisters and refused to believe that he could not find a job. When the brickyards were working he would be in line at four in the morning to get a day's work. He swept streets, picked cherries, went down on his knees with Mexican transient laborers in the sugar-beet fields, and, by accepting anything that came along, managed to provide for his sisters. The days on which he could find no work were spent in the parsonage studying in father's library. Side by side, Ronald and father read by the hour, neither disturbing the other. Ronald's courage inspired father to scour the entire county for work the young man could do. But after each expedition father walked the floor.

"There must be some way we can put that lad back in law school," he fretted. "This depression is burying the genius of an entire generation."

One afternoon when father saw Ronald approaching the house he went to the kitchen, where mother was baking.

"Mother," he said, "I don't think Ronald ever has enough to eat. But every time I invite him to stay for dinner he declines. I think he's too proud to admit he's hungry. Will you bring in a generous sample of your cookies when they're out of the oven? And put some apples on the plate, too."

Mother complied, and all afternoon father watched from the corner of his eyes while, one by one, ten cookies and three apples disappeared. From that time on he always had a midafternoon snack for himself, which Ronald shared ravenously.

After nearly a year of this, father's heart could stand no

more of Ronald's suffering. One afternoon he walked into
the office of the most prominent lawyer in town, a man
who went to no church.

"George," father said, "you have enjoyed being a pa-
gan long enough. I've got a job for you."

George Hardy smiled.

"What's the trouble, Dr. Spence?" he asked. "Somebody suing you for alienation of affections?"

"It's Ronald McCarren, George," father continued.
"You know the lad, I think. He wants to be a lawyer.
You've made enough money from the law—legally
and illegally—that you can afford to give this boy an
education."

He talked for ten minutes, reviewing Ronald's history,
his ability, and his courage. At the conclusion, Hardy
held out his hand.

"Dr. Spence," he promised, "we'll do it. Damn it to
Hell, the kid needs a break! You find a home for the
girls, and I'll see Ronald through."

From Laketon, Morningside, and Fort Dodge, men
and women in trouble came to consult their former
pastor. People drove as many as two hundred miles to be
advised or comforted by him, sometimes remaining
overnight with us.

In one of his first charges father had known a banker
who lived in unusual splendor but who had been generous to his church. The great bank crash caught him,
and he fled to escape arrest. A fugitive from justice, under
indictment for malfeasance and without a penny in his
pocket, the banker knocked at our back door late one
night. Father admitted and sheltered him for a week,

during which he raised enough money among his friends to enable the banker to return home, furnish bail, and exonerate himself in a public trial.

Living so intimately with his congregation, father almost inevitably came to modify his ideas regarding personal conduct. He laughed heartily when, in the course of pastoral calls, he walked one day into a bridge party. The hostess was embarrassed, but father put her at ease immediately.

"Don't look at me as though you had been caught whipping a dog," he said. "Since you women have forgotten how to sew you've got to have some excuse to gossip."

And when a timid mother came begging him to advise her daughter against accepting a job in New York, father replied, "It's a job, isn't it? What's the trouble?"

"I can't bear to think of Nancy going so far away all by herself," the mother answered. "Think what might happen to her!"

"Mrs. Knowles," father said, "did you ever think what might happen to her in an Iowa haystack?"

Calls came at all hours. One night he was summoned by a physician to the bedside of a member of his church.

"Dr. Spence," Dr. Horn told him just outside the sickroom, "I've done everything in the world I can for this man. He has pneumonia, complicated by a gastric ulcer. But he has a strong constitution and should pull through. His trouble is that he doesn't want to live. Unless you can do something he's going to die."

Father entered the sickroom and sat beside the patient.

"Well, Bob," he said, "you're looking better."

The patient was not deceived.

Father began to talk about a church problem, but there was no response. So he turned his monologue into praise of Bob Graham's sons and daughters, all in high school: of his pride that the father had accomplished so much with his children; of the future in store for these children in a world of radio and airplanes and Cellophane. He made the prospects so bright that the patient began to listen.

"You're lucky, Bob. You have nursed your children through their most trying days. Now you can sit back and watch them develop. The most wonderful years of a father's life are those when he watches his daughters become women and marry and begin their own family lives; when his son steps out into the world to make a name for himself. Soon the father is a grandfather and becomes a young man again in spirit. The best years of your life lie ahead. And you are going to run away from them."

Graham stirred.

"Yes, you are," father went on. "You are going to run out on them. Who will walk down the aisle with your daughters when they are married? No one, for you will be gone. Who will encourage your son when his days are difficult, and give him the benefit of your experience? No one. You'll be gone. Business is tough, and you think you're going bankrupt, and you want to die. Other men will weather it somehow and come out into the sunlight again. But not you. You're the man who let his children down. You couldn't take it. So you quit."

The patient turned his head. "Don't, Doc," he said. "I'm not quitting."

"Yes, you are, Bob. Dr. Horn says the only thing that's

killing you is your desire to die. You're quitting. You're going to leave a bankruptcy for your wife to settle. She'll have to fight alone. What does she know of business? You're not playing fair with her for being a good wife and a good mother. It's a dirty trick, Bob."

Again the patient squirmed. "Please don't, Doc," he begged. "I can't take it."

"That's why I'm here, because you can't take it. What's the matter with you anyway? Isn't there any fight left in you?"

Graham shook his head.

"Then find some," father urged. "Isn't it enough that you have messed up your own life without passing that burden on to your children? Do you want them to remember you as the man who quit when the going was tough?"

"No."

"Do you want to leave them alone in the world? You know it's a hard world without making it any harder for them. Are you being fair?"

"Please, Doc, don't."

"Then pull yourself together, man!"

Graham drew up his chest and breathed more deeply.

"That's the spirit. Once more, breathe."

The patient rallied.

"And once again."

Graham collapsed.

"Come on," father coaxed, going to the bed and taking him by the shoulders. "Fight. You've got to live. We're going to win this battle, Bob. Now, breathe."

Bob Graham breathed.

"Again."

The patient made a greater effort.

"Again."

He tried a little harder.

"That's it. Breathe, man, breathe!"

For an hour the battle went on, father encouraging his patient the while. Occasionally Dr. Horn entered the room for a quick ministration, then vanished. Long after midnight Graham's pulse rate steadied, his respirations eased. But he was exhausted.

Dr. Horn, looked across the bed at father, nodded. Father stepped aside. A few moments later Graham was asleep.

Father took up sentry duty outside the partly open door. Occasionally the patient moaned. Instantly father was at his side.

"Fight, man," he would whisper fiercely, "fight."

Toward morning father was haggard. Dr. Horn handed him a cigar. "It will help to keep you awake," he said.

Father's impulse was to refuse. He had never smoked. But he was terribly tired.

"What do you do with the blooming thing?" he asked.

Following instructions, he bit the end and lit the cigar. For a long time he smoked quietly. There was no further sound from the sickroom.

"I think everything is all right," he told Dr. Horn as daylight reminded him of his fatigue. "Call if I'm needed."

He went home. About noon he returned to the Graham house and found the patient much improved. In mid-afternoon Dr. Horn telephoned.

"How's our patient?" he asked.

Father chuckled, made his report, and restored the telephone to its cradle.

"Mother," he called excitedly upstairs, "Dr. Horn just phoned. He wanted to know how *our* patient is getting along."

28

~~~~~

FATHER's heart held out until the congregation had shaken off the bitterest years of the economic depression. Then he was stricken.

One week end I went to Mason City from Des Moines, where I was working, and father and I sat up late Saturday night, for him an unusual concession. The next morning he was exhausted and not well but went to church as usual. When he saw me sitting in the pew beside mother, after an absence of several months, emotional excitement further increased his cardiac distress. He was very pale and in pain as he entered the pulpit. Mother gripped my hand and held it tightly. All went well, however, until the responsive reading. Then he did something he had never done before. The reading covered two pages of the Psalter, and, in turning the page, he accidentally turned two. At any other time he would have realized his mistake immediately. But this morning all his attention was concentrated on the physical task of remaining on his feet. He read his response, but the congregation, instead of reading aloud after him, remained silent. Father did not know what to do.

"Dr. Spence," Frank Curry, a board member, called, "I believe you have turned two pages instead of one."

Father flipped back a page and continued calmly. After that, holding onto the pulpit to keep from falling, he delivered a sermon from which he did not cut a single word. We had to help him home and into bed.

By midafternoon he rallied. But he knew, now, that he must be constantly on guard and that any undue exertion would fell him. He did not say so, of course. He put on his lounging robe and went to the library, where he was most at home.

"Look at this room," he said wistfully. "When I die there won't be much of an estate. But what a priceless legacy that library would be to any son of mine who entered the ministry."

He had given up hope that I would be a preacher, and Fraser, now a college senior, was taking a salesmanship course.

"I wish I were a young preacher today," he went on, settling into the monologue style I had grown to know so well. "What I could do! All the hidebound old rules are gone. A preacher can be a human being, now."

He looked at me as though hoping I might still change my mind and follow his career. But I could only remain silent.

"Young men don't have to be afraid of the ministry these days. A lot of ideas we used to have don't mean much any more."

He gazed out at the passing traffic.

"Look at that line of automobiles, everyone hurrying to

Clear Lake. When I first came to this country I used to think it was sinful for a man to spend his Sunday at a cottage, swimming and amusing himself. Now I know that a lake can be a great spiritual consolation to a man and that a little swimming doesn't profane the Sabbath. God wants his children to keep themselves physically fit."

A look of amazement crossed his face, as though he recognized for the first time just how far his attitude had changed.

"There goes Roger Hansen, walking to work," he went on, calling particular attention to a passer-by. "I remember the time I preached a sermon on the evil of Sunday employment. These days a man is lucky to have a job at all, even on Sunday. He must take what he can get. When I preached that sermon against Sunday employment I was right; nobody needed to work on Sunday then. Last week I advised Roger to take this Sunday job."

He paused while the fingers of his right hand sought the pulse of his left to clock the telltale extra systoles that were so disturbing.

"You will recall," he resumed, "that at Riverton I let you take a Sunday-morning paper route because you had no respect for your Sunday-school teacher. It was better for you to be working happily than to be developing a habit of rebellion against religion."

He smiled. "I don't even say a man must go to church *every* Sunday. If I were not a preacher I'd probably skip a few Sundays myself. But I'd go often on week days. Going only to a Sunday-morning service is not sufficient to revitalize a man. Civilization is so quickly paced we no longer have time to think or meditate. And God suffers. Christians should get the habit of dropping in at their church every day on their way to work or on their way home or during the noon hour. Five minutes would be enough to compose their troubled spirits. God would be pleased that we remembered Him, even if only for a minute."

"I think more people are doing that now," I interrupted. "Not many, but a few."

"Well," he said, "that's encouraging. I remarked a moment ago that it is better to be working on the Sabbath than developing a habit of rebellion against religion. I should not have said religion. I should have used the word Christianity. Religion means many things; Christianity, only one. Our Leader deserves the recognition that we are not just religious, but Christian."

Again he looked at me, and I knew he was trying to persuade me to enter the ministry.

"What a wonderful world this is for you children," he exclaimed. "Your approach to Christianity and that of my day are as different as the New Testament from the Old. But you should not abuse your new conception of Christ's loving kindness. It is all right to go to a baseball game on Sunday if you can't go during the week. The relaxation is good for you. But you should not disrespect the Sabbath with baseball or fishing or motion pictures or other pleasures *if* you are able to pursue them during the week."

He chuckled. "I'm afraid my thinking has come a long way. But then so has that of the church."

He asked me to hand him a copy of the latest Methodist Discipline, which was on his desk.

"Look here," he said. "When I became a preacher a Methodist could not sue another. Quarrels were unchristian. Now the church concedes the authority of the state along with the authority of God. In line with that we have relaxed our rules about divorce. Thirty years ago there was only one ground for divorce recognized by Christian people, and no minister would think of remarrying a divorced person unless he was the injured party in an adulterous marriage. Now we admit it is the function of the state to determine the grounds on which a divorce may be allowed and recognize as legal any divorce granted by the state. We receive divorced persons into the church these days.

"Formerly we never dared even whisper any sexual instruction to young people. Now our Discipline advises pastors to teach the young and prepare them for their marital obligations, even suggesting medical examinations. That's quite a step."

He closed the Discipline.

"Yes, Christianity has become something to *live*, not just something to believe in the abstract."

A few months later, when I returned home for my vacation, the fact that no son of his was a clergyman was still in father's mind. He was up and at work again, and we were alone, for mother was visiting Eileen in Denver. By this time I was smoking, and father still disapproved. Actually I had begun to smoke in high school, and father knew it, but even now he would not allow me to smoke in his presence or anywhere in the house.

Out of deference I would go out on the porch and light my pipe. Father ignored my smoking the first two or three days. He would wait in the living room until I knocked out the ash, then join me. But he was naturally too talkative to tolerate that very long. One night he came onto the porch just after I had lighted up. Immediately I set the pipe aside.

"Oh, that's all right, son," he said. "Since you're not going to be a preacher, I guess there's no harm in it."

We began to discuss his sermon of the previous Sunday, when suddenly he stepped off the porch and bought something from a little girl who was passing. Guiltily he put his purchase in his pocket. When he returned he did not mention it.

The next week the identical scene occurred. This time I asked what he was up to.

"You know Father Reilly's dog," he laughed.

I had often admired the dog, a magnificent Saint Bernard that followed the priest everywhere. The Catholic rectory was just around the corner, and the priest and father were good friends.

"Well," he resumed, "every week the women's guild raffles off that dog, and every week whoever wins it goes to Father Reilly and gives it back. I've been trying to win that dog for six weeks. I think it would be fun."

Autumn began father's last year in the ministry. At first he was still able to preach on Sunday, but during the week he remained at home, and the congregation brought both church and personal problems to him. He did all he could to unravel them.

Mother's problem, however, he couldn't solve. After four years in Mason City she was again in the Sunday school, leading the juniors. But Mason City was very conscious of its public school program. The high school band had won several national honors. The orchestra and chorus were state leaders. The high schools had absorbed the town's musical talent. None remained for the church.

Mother was indignant.

"My music is as important as that of the schools," she told father.

"Oh, no, it isn't, mother," he smiled, "you haven't won three national championships."

Mother never solved her problem. A few days later father suffered a coronary thrombosis that kept him invalid for a year. But even though he could not lead his people, they refused for eleven months to accept a new pastor. Father's salary continued, and from it he paid a theological student to come out from Chicago and conduct the Sunday services. Twice he begged the official board to replace him, but the members refused.

The hundreds he had befriended came to comfort him. His room constantly was filled with flowers. Parishioners, acquaintances, and friends from all over North Iowa came to sit by his bedside. His nonchurch guests would exclaim at the many flowers his congregation sent.

"I was their depression pastor," father would explain simply.

He continued to be keenly interested in all church affairs. He was delighted when, at the city election, a majority of the councilmen elected were Methodists, although the mayor was a Catholic. Father wrote to the mayor, offering to donate a picture of Methodism's founder, John Wesley, for the council chamber. The mayor answered by sending a box of roses.

Father even learned to play euchre. Eileen, home for a

vacation, taught him. Cards, which had never been allowed in the parsonage, were now frequently spread out on father's bed.

When November came he listened eagerly to football broadcasts. One Saturday afternoon the son of an old friend telephoned from the courthouse, asking if father was strong enough to perform a wedding ceremony.

Father thought quickly, then asked him to come to the parsonage in twenty minutes. He figured that by then the football game would have reached the half-time intermission. He was right. Propped up in a chair, he read the wedding service and hustled the bride and groom out of the house before the game was resumed.

The next week end his condition suddenly became more serious. I, being nearest of the children, hurried home.

But I found father laughing, though he could scarcely move. "If you came for the obsequies," he challenged as I entered the room, "I am happy to disappoint you."

He seemed to gain strength during my brief stay. Guiltily I told him that I had left my work without reporting to Chicago and that when my superiors discovered my absence I might be in difficulty.

"Then you mustn't stay," he said at once. "Your life has a long uphill run ahead, and your work is important. Mine is coasting downgrade and what's left of it isn't worth any risks."

But he was happy to talk on and on, principally about my future. He wanted to be sure that my home training was so strong that without him I could go on alone.

"You are an egotistical youngster," he said at one point, "but don't worry too much about that. Someone

will come along at the proper time and pin your ears
back. You just go on about your work with everything
that's in you and trust in God, and you'll be all right.
But don't run up and down stairs, or put your heart to
needless excitement."

He kept looking at me as though he were never going
to see me again and wanted something to remember.

"A little egotism is a good thing. I have often been
called egotistical myself. It used to worry me. But one
day in the mountains I figured it out. I respect myself.
That is a good thing. A man must respect himself first if
he is to command respect from others."

We talked on and on. As always, he returned to a discussion of the church.

"I was reading an article the other day," he said,
"which purported to show that the church is slipping. I
was very impatient. This writer argued that ministers are
preaching to half-empty churches, that nobody practices
Christianity any more. That's all nonsense. Look at this
church. Did you ever see a better? No. Did you ever see a
more active congregation? No. Did you ever see a finer
set of Christian people? No. We have three churches
within an area of two blocks: our own, the Catholic, and
the Christian Scientist. Stand on the corner any Sunday
when those three churches are holding service, and you'll
see that cars can't get within four blocks of here because
of the crowd. Christianity dying, humbug! Christianity
is just beginning to live. It doesn't make such a *show* any
more. I admit. The old revival meeting is gone, the prayer
meeting is gone, the camp meeting is gone. People are
more Christian in their *homes* and in their *hearts*. Look at
the figures in any almanac, and you'll see that the mem-

bership of Christian churches continually increases, year after year. Don't let anybody fool you about Christianity. It's still very much alive. If God thought His church was in any danger, He would come to its rescue."

The telephone rang. I answered. The call was from Chicago, informing me that I had been transfered to New York and must leave immediately. Quickly I told father and looked up bus schedules. I just had time to catch the last bus that day.

As I turned to leave father held out both his hands and took mine. His grasp was firm.

"Son," he said, "I am very happy over your promotion. I like to be proud of my sons. You are going far away. When you return, I probably will not be here."

He caught his breath.

"But don't worry about me. We are both moving up to new jobs. You know that you are going to New York; and, just as surely, I know where I am going. You know what to expect when you get there; so, too, do I."

His clear eyes held mine for a long moment. I could not reply. We both knew we would not see each other again.

"God bless you, son," he said, "good-by."

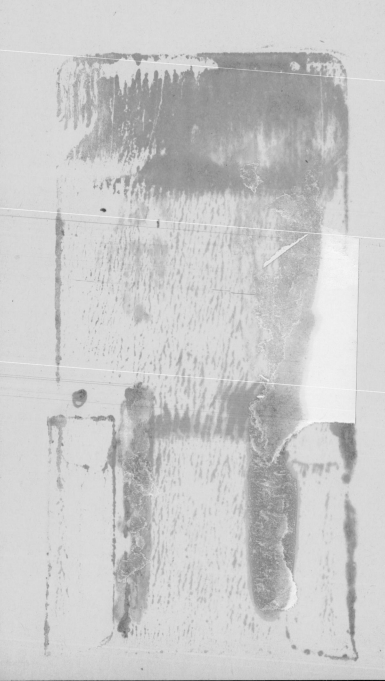